Dutch Oven Cookin'

By

Dick Stucki

Including recipes from the Old Deseret Cookoff
Cover Photo by Dick Stucki

Published by
Bonneville Publishing Co.
Division of Life Institute Inc.
P. O. Box 65552
Salt Lake City, Utah, 84165-0552

NOTICE: The information contained in this book is true and complete to the best of our knowledge. All recommendations are made without any guarantees on the part of the author or Bonneville Publishing Co. or Life Institute Inc. The author and publisher disclaim all liability in connection with the use of this information.

The book is dedicated to my wonderful wife, Pamela who stands by my side in all I do and encourages and inspires me. She has spent many hours helping with the production of this book. A more wonderful wife no man could ask for. And to my mother Mary Koehler who taught me to cook as a child and let me experiment and create as I cooked. Without her teaching, I would not be where I am. I would also like to remember the many terrific friends that have made Dutch oven cooking so much fun over the years and who have shared recipes with us so freely.

Dutch oven cooking can be a great adventure, wether cooking for your family or a large group as shown above. Stew for the Masses (page 85) is shown above using 2 - 17" ovens in front followed by 2 - 22" ovens, then many 12" & 14" ovens filled with cobbler for desert.

Table of Contents

Dick Stucki tastes dish being prepared for a large group, while his wife, Pam, stirs another oven.

About The Author

Dick Stucki has been cooking for fun ever since he was a young boy, and learned to use the Dutch oven while a Boy Scout. From that time on, he has been cooking in Dutch ovens and sharing his good food and ideas with anyone wanting to learn.

A fully qualified chef in his own right, Dick has been competing in cooking competitions for the past 12 years, and winning in most of the competitions he cooks in. Among them are the Farm Bureau Cookout King, Showmanship Champion and Dutch Oven Champion for Utah. He has won numerous competitions in many county cookoffs, and has won many prizes in the World Championship of Dutch Oven Cooking.

Many people have had the privilege of eating his cooking and learning from him either in classes he teaches, or at demonstrations he has given for various groups and churches.

He also regularly cooks for large groups catering dinners for churches, families and companies.

Cooking in a Dutch oven does not usually require a large number of briquets. The oven above is baking at about 350 F. with 6 - 8 coals on the bottom and 14 - 18 on top.

One of the most popular desserts is cobbler. The cobbler above is ready for cooking. The oven is lined with foil. You see the brown sugar dotted with butter which will blend together to make the delicious topping.

Forward

Dutch oven cooking is a special activity that can be enjoyed by all. The fun not only comes in eating, but also on the way to the finished product. Dutch oven cooking is the perfect way to entertain. I love to have friends over to help with the preparation of a Dutch oven meal.

We start by frying chicken to crispy brown. I then have the children add the tomato sauce and mushrooms. While the pot is cooking for an hour we simmer with fun conversation and end up with a delicious pot of Pistol Rock Chicken. Fun is enjoyed by all.

Dick has prepared many special recipes which await your touch. He has included many hints for you to try and enjoy. I have had the opportunity of judging many of Dick's dishes and have found them delightful.

You can have many hours of family fun and entertainment by sitting around a Dutch oven waiting for your special pot to simmer. Have fun Dutching.

Dian Thomas,
Author, *Roughing It Easy*

Don't be afraid to set an elegant table, even when cooking out doors. You and your guests deserve it.

"This book will take you from novice to gourmet Dutch oven cook"

We started cooking in Dutch ovens in 1974. Our first try resulted in a 10-inch oven full of burnt, black potatoes. We argued the responsibility of clean-up from that disaster for several months, each determined not to scrub that oven. We both won and the oven lost. It remained on the side porch for several years, six to be exact. At that time, we started working with the Scouting program. During a training session, we watched a simple cooking demonstration involving a Dutch oven and the results were so delicious, we gave the 10-inch oven the "burned-out" treatment, reseasoned it and went to work developing our own cooking skills with this fascinating black pot.

During this time we purchased several "how to" books. Some offered just the basics, others were more advanced. Every author has a idea of how cooking with a Dutch oven should be done. Few offered a full spectrum. With these facts in mind we read through Dick Stucki's new cookbook, *Dutch Oven Cookin'*, and were delighted to find something we had looked for in other books; enough variety and methods to take and person from a novice to a gourmet Dutch oven cook.

We have cooked against Dick and his wife Pam in many Dutch oven cookoffs, and with them for Scout groups, church groups, family groups, and Dutch oven cooking classes. While they are creative, innovative and challenging, they have always maintained the spirit of friendly competition by sharing secrets, encouraging new comers, and supporting anyone needing help, like helping us carry our 22", 149 pound Dutch oven to the judges during a contest requiring the ovens be presented at the judges table.

Dick has carried the same qualities and enthusiasm into his book on Dutch oven cooking. He shared within its covers, over ten years of hard work and experience that have made him a champion cook.

Joan and Than Larsen

Portable camp kitchens are a valuable tool for the outdoor cook. You will see several different designs in this book. They can hold all the spices and cooking ingredients that you use as well as having a bread board surface for working on. If you are a handyman-type, you may want to design and build one to suit your needs.

Introduction

Every year during the summer, you can see large numbers of city dwellers head for the hills to go fishing, camping, hunting, hiking and even for picnics.

The one thing they all have in common, is that most of them will be hungry and want to have something to eat. The question is usually what to eat. Some will have very simple lunches or dinners and some will even survive only on snack foods they take along. But you could have one of the most enjoyable dinners if you plan and take along a Dutch oven.

After using Dutch ovens or camp Dutch ovens as some call them, for the past 25 years or so, I am convinced that most people could eat better when out in the hills or at the picnic grounds if they would just try a new way of cooking.

Many people are finding that Dutch ovens can give you one of the most enjoyable experiences. About the only thing better when you are out camping or at a picnic would be eating what you have just fixed.

No matter if the meal is for your own family or a group of friends, you will really enjoy this way of cooking. After you get hooked on cooking with a Dutch oven, you will be trying to find excuses to use your Dutch ovens continually.

Cast iron has been around a long time. In fact, for centuries. Early settlers who came to America brought black iron pots with them and used them as their primary cooking utensil. When Lewis and Clark made their famous expedition to the Northwest, they depended upon the tried and true Dutch oven.

In the early days of the West, the black iron Dutch oven played a very important role. To the mountain man it was one of his most prized possessions in which he cooked stews and wild game to perfection in his black iron kettle.

The pioneers who came across the plains to the Rocky Mountains also prized their Dutch ovens. As they traveled to Utah, California and Oregon, they always had a Dutch oven on their wagons. Sometimes it would be tied on the side of the wagon, or perhaps you would find it swinging from the tailgate of the wagon, but you could count on finding at least one.

Another important part of the early history of the West was the numerous cattle drives that went across the country in the late 1800's. Nearly every drive had a chuckwagon which followed along to feed the cowhands, and they always had several Dutch ovens stored in the "boot" of the wagon.

In later years the Dutch oven became the standby utensil for the sheepherder. He would cook his lamb stews, sourdough breads and dishes famous of the Basque.

Dutch oven cooking is more than just dumping food in a black pot and putting it on the fire hoping that it will be good to eat. Choose the type of cooking that fits the food and you will have much better results.

There are several types of cooking you can do in

the Dutch oven. Some are stewing or boiling, steaming, roasting, baking, poaching and frying. Each of these types of cooking have their place depending on the recipe. Learn to use them all and your group or family will enjoy your cooking even more.

Probably the biggest mistake people make, is not realizing the possibilities available to them with a Dutch oven. When I was first exposed to cooking with the Dutch oven, the only thing I saw was chicken or cobbler or mutton stew. While these are still good items everyone should know and use, they are by no means a stopping place for any cook. I still like those dishes, but I've discovered that there are a great many other dishes that are tasty also. So don't be afraid to try something new, and before long you will be coming up with ideas of your own.

You can cook anything in your Dutch oven that you would normally cook in your home oven, like bread, rolls, homemade pies, pizza, crown roasts, meatloafs, lobster and even prime rib. I have never tasted anything that didn't seem to taste better cooked in a Dutch oven. The recipes that are in this book include some basic starters, some intermediate dishes and a few advanced recipes for you to try and enjoy. As you become more proficient at Dutch oven cooking, you will become aware of the scope of recipes available to you which will leave your family and guests in awe. Remember, anything that can be fried, boiled, baked, steamed or poached, can be cooked in a Dutch oven.

Another important point in favor of the Dutch oven is its versatility in times of emergency. Just think, if your power or gas were off for a prolonged period of time, you could still fix great meals for your family using your Dutch ovens. That is a comforting thought. So as you use your Dutch ovens regularly, you will be able to become proficient enough to do just that.

The Dutch oven has another great feature. You can take off the lid and turn it upsidedown and level it on three rocks or bricks, and use it like a griddle or crepe pan. This way you can cook bacon and eggs, hot cakes, french toast, or even fancy crepe.

Next time you have a group of friends over instead of getting out the old barbecue, try a Dutch oven dish and find out how much your guests like it.

If you would like to see some great cooking and get some great ideas for your Dutch oven, I would recommend that you go to one of the many competitions that are held each year. There is always a cookoff for dutch ovens at Old Deseret in Pioneer Trails State Park, in Salt Lake City, Utah on July 24th. Those recipes are included in this book. There are many other cookoffs across the country including the Farm Bureau Cookout King contests and many other cooking events including pie contests, chili cookoffs, sourdough cookoffs, Beef Council cookoffs, and many others. Visit a few, and you will surely broaden your horizons. Watch the wide variety of dishes being prepared. If you like gourmet cooking try some of these new ideas.

What ever the case may be, I hope you will try some of the recipes in this book and find out how good you can eat whether you are in your own backyard or in the hills. Just remember to Enjoy!!

Part 1

Getting Started with the Dutch Oven

A wind break is a handy tool to have around. The one above is made of sheet metal. Wind is one of the most unpredictable elements of nature. At the left of the windbreak are two gallon cans. Vent holes have been punched around the bottom. This is one way to start charcoal Briquets.

The Dutch oven lis is a very handy cooking surface. By placing it upside down on bricks or rocks you can use it as a griddle to saute vegetables, cook meats, crepes, pancakes, eggs, etc.

Chapter 1

Some Basics of Dutch Oven Cooking

"NOTES"

Selecting and Buying a Dutch Oven

A camp Dutch oven is made of cast iron. It is a pot with a flat bottom and the lid has a flange around the outside of it which helps hold the coals while cooking. Because it is made out of cast iron it will heat evenly with very little heat.

In the early pioneer days, the families considered their Dutch oven as one of their most valuable possessions. The same was true for the mountainmen. You will find this a valuable tool for cooking in your yard or in the hills. As a valuable tool you should take some care in selecting the oven because they will last for many years if taken care of.

When you shop for a new Dutch oven, you should be aware that all ovens are not the same. There are ovens ranging in size from eight inches in diameter to 22 inches in diameter. And there are various depths available. Most average families start out with 12 or 14 inch ovens and then add ovens to meet their particular needs.

A few of the things to watch out for follow: I would check the fit of the lid. You want it to fit well. The lid, during cooking will make a seal and turn the oven into a form of pressure cooker, so the fit is very important. Check the oven finish and be sure that it is not uneven. The walls should be the same thickness all the way around. There are some new imported ovens on the market where the wall are not even. I would avoid any oven that doesn't look even and of good quality. It may break and surely will not heat evenly. The surface should be an even gray color and should not show too many signs of grinding where they have had to fix imperfections. Remember the old adage, "you get what you pay for." This hold true with dutch ovens in the same way it does for many other products.

You will notice that the bail or handle sets different on one side of the oven from the other. When you are cooking with the oven you should try to keep the bail in the position which holds it up above the level of the lid. When you are storing the oven put the handle in the lower position. You want the handle in the upper position while cooking to keep it away from the fire so it won't overheat the bail causing it to bend.

Seasoning the New Dutch Oven

Well, you just bought your first Dutch oven and the clerk at the store told you to remember and season it before you use it. And the clerk is right.

We will now embark on an area of Dutch oven cooking that you will hear a lot about.

I am sure that if you asked 100 Dutch oven cooks how to season an oven you will probably get 100 different answers.

When you are seasoning a new oven, Lodge Manufacturing Co. recommends the following procedure:

1. Warm the Dutch oven and peel off the label.

2. Wash, rinse and dry thoroughly. Use mild, soapy water (NEVER an abrasive detergent) and a stiff brush.

3. Grease the Dutch oven with a thin coating of vegetable oil or fat. Do not use salad fat (margarine or butter). Warm the oven and then spread oil or fat over the entire surface with cloth or paper towel. Be certain that the entire surface of the oven has been coated thoroughly.

4. Place the oven in your home oven and heat to 300 - 350 degrees for 30 - 60 minutes. Allow the oven to remain in the oven until it cools to room

temperature.   This completes the seasoning process.

Other cooks have good ideas also.   One friend of mine uses his gas barbecue to heat up the ovens to about 400 degrees.   He then pulls them off the heat and wipes a thin coat of oil over the entire surface rubbing the oil in until it quits smoking. He then returns the oven to the heat.   He repeats this process as many as 10 or 12 times until his ovens have a heavy seasoning and they shine like they have been sprayed with a high-gloss lacquer.

I have many times just used a good old camp fire to heat up my ovens with oil in them.   When the oil is hot, spread the oil around the oven with a lint free cloth, coating the entire surface of the oven.   I like to use the oven for the first time with an entree that will be cooked in oil such as chicken. This will help in the seasoning of the oven.

Remember that the most important thing is that you do season it.   It is the seasoning on the oven that protects it from rusting while not in use and it is also the feature that gives your oven a stick-free surface.

If you haven't used your oven for some time, and it smells that way (rancid), you can re-season your oven and bring it back into service.   Just start over again with the seasoning process.   Wipe out your oven, heat it up again and oil it good.   Then enjoy the good cooking.

Cleaning Your Dutch Oven

I like to clean my ovens right after I use them whenever possible.   You can clean your oven by first scraping out any leftover residue from your cooking, then put it back on the heat.   Let it go until all of the food that was left is burnt free, and then scrape it clean. After you have the oven clean, oil it and store it for your next use. This is the same idea as a self cleaning oven.

Another way we clean our ovens (especially if you have been cooking with sugary foods) is to wash it out with a very mild soapy water. Then while still hot, coat with oil like you did when you were seasoning it. One tip is to not put too heavy of a coat of oil at any one time. It will just get sticky. Keep it thin.

You will have to try some of the various ways of cleaning your ovens to find out which way you prefer to do it, just like you will have to try a few different ways of seasoning your ovens before you decide on a way that is right for you.

If your Dutch oven gets rusty, just clean off all the rust you can and then rub with oil, heat it and rub with oil some more, then re-season it as before.

Storing Your Dutch Oven

After you finish a meal and the ovens are cool and ready for storage, you want to take some precautions in storing them.

Store your ovens with the lids a-jar. This will let the air circulate and you should try to keep them in a warm dry place. you can also put a piece of newspaper wadded up inside which will help absorb any moisture that build up.

Always be careful with your Dutch ovens. They are breakable, so don't drop them or bang them into other hard surfaces. Treat them like glass and you will be safe.

When your oven is hot, never add cold water to it or it might break just like a glass bowl would.

Take care of your ovens and they will last your lifetime.

Choosing the Right Size Oven

Dutch ovens today are available in a variety of sizes. You can get ovens ranging from 8 inch to 22 inch and the depths of the ovens will run from about 3 inches deep to nearly 12 inches deep. As you can see, with that kind of variety to choose from, you want to get the right one for the right job.

One of the most frequently asked questions is "what size oven should I buy?" I would suggest that if you are starting out, get a 12 or 14 inch oven. I feel these are the most versatile ovens to start with. You can then add other ovens of different sizes as you can afford to and have a need.

The following chart should give you a good idea of the different sizes with their capacities and ideas of how I've used them in cooking. I hope it will be helpful for you. I'm sure there are other uses also.

Oven Size	Oven Capacity	Some Ideas for Uses
8"	2 qts	Baked apples, beans, vegetables
10"	4 qts	Baked bread, cakes, beans, rolls
12"	6 qts	Main dishes 12 -14 people, cobbler
13"	14 qts	Deep oven. Roast, stews, cakes.
14"	8 qts	Main dishes 16 -20 people, cobbler
15"	16 qts	Deep oven. Bundt cakes, roasts, ribs.
16"	12 qts	Dishes for large groups,
17"	30 qts	Deep oven. Big dishes, crown roast,
22"	68 qts	Giant groups, prime rib, stews

Two variations of buckets to start briquets are shown above. On the left is an old railroad box car heater, while on the right is a 5 gallon bucket that has been designed with a grate 6' above the bottom of the bucket.

Windbreaks can be made in a variety of ways. Above is one made from a 55 gallon drum. When the wind is not a problem, the sides can be removed.

Dutch Oven Cooking Tools

You have your ovens and they are seasoned, now you want to get cooking. First, let's talk about some of the tools you will want to have to make your job easier. There are a few tools that will help you as you work with your Dutch ovens.

You will need a shovel, when working with a wood fire. This is to get the coals out of the fire pit and place them on the oven. If working with a real fire, you will want to have an ax handy to help in preparing the wood for the fire.

Since the National Forest Service has discouraged using open fires in most areas, and the fact that it is more work to prepare a wood fire, most Dutch oven cooks have gone to using charcoal briquets. It is also easier to control the temperature of the oven using charcoal briquets, and I would recommend them, but please buy the best brand you can afford. Again, this is a case where you will get what you pay for. I have used most brands, some were terrible some so-so, and some great. I personally recommend Kingsford. I have never had a problem with it and is available in most stores.

Probably the most useful tools you will have are tongs. Get a long pair. Either regular barbecue tongs or go to the restaurant supply and get some long tongs from them. You will want to have two pair. One for handling food while cooking, and one pair for moving coals to the oven.

You can take some regular home cooking tools and extend the handles with dowels or the like and they will be helpful additions to your camp kitchen tool set. You will continually get ideas of ways to make things. Don't be afraid to try some of them, you may hit on a great idea.

Tools to help make Dutch oven cooking easier are available in many types. Above you will see a cooking table, lid stand, lifting tools and Dutch oven storage bag all made commercially.

Many tools can be made by the do-it-yourselfer. From the left, is a homemade lid stand, wire basket for starting briquets and a lid lifting tool made in a home shop. All are very functional and useful

Another essential tool you will need is a lifting tool. There are lots of different ideas here also. There is an all-aluminum lifting tool designed to go under the lid handle and still keep the oven stable. This is a good one. It is made by Gales, in St. George, Utah. Another set comes with a short tool and a long tool for lifting. You can use them individually or as a set for pouring. Another lifter can be made from a hoe handle with a hook bolted on to it. The important thing is to have a tool to make the lifting of the hot lid and oven easier. Any of these tools, some of which are commercially available, will aid you in lifting the ovens. They hook on the bail and you lift with the tool. This way you will not burn yourself.

A good pair of leather gloves are always good to have. After you have been cooking with coals, either wood or briquets, you will want a whisk broom to sweep off the ashes. This will make your oven look much more presentable when your present your food or serve it up to your guests.

Other items you will want to keep on hand are some cotton rags, cooking oil for cleaning your oven, and perhaps a charcoal bucket to start your coals in.

I would recommend a special box to keep your tools in so you will have them ready when you want to cook. An old milk crate works great for this, and you can turn it over on its side and use it like a shelf while you are preparing your foods.

Cooking In Your Yard

It would be a real shame for anyone with a Dutch oven to miss one of the greatest opportunities to use their Dutch ovens. At home. That's right, out in your back yard. So often families go out back to have a barbecue, and they settle for hamburgers, steaks, or chicken. Well, you could also have that cookout using your Dutch ovens. This will open up a whole new realm of possibilities of dishes you can fix. Don't be afraid to experiment. I think that every dish you could name would taste better prepared in a Dutch oven. And you can even use your barbecue to heat your Dutch oven if you wish at home. That is your choice. But please try a dutch oven dish next time the family or friends get together.

You will want to, if at all possible, select a regular place to cook with your dutch ovens. You may have a spot just off your patio where you could put a small square of cinder block pavers to cook on. This will give you a place to put your coals. You can level the spot when your put in the pavers so you will know that your ovens will always be level when you cook there.

Another idea that I have used is to cut off the bottom of a 55 gallon drum and use it to put the coals in and hold the ovens. I like to place it on two full sized cinder blocks. Or you can have some legs welded to the base to make a permanent stand. I have found that about 12 - 16 inches off the ground is about as high as you will want to go to allow you to maintain good leverage with your lifting tools when removing the lids to work in the ovens.

You can even get very elaborate and build a complete brick Dutch oven barbecue pit area. Put benches around and have a major party area. Or how about a fire pit made inside an old wagon wheel rim? Or just line the rim of the fire pit with rocks.

Whatever method you choose, I am sure it will make your cooking in the yard easier, and an enjoyable experience.

Fires For Dutch Oven Cooking

You can heat your Dutch oven for cooking in a number of ways. You can use a gas grill, barbecue, even your home range, but most likely you will settle on either wood fire or charcoal briquets.

Remember though, you don't have to use a very hot fire all the time. The design of the cast iron Dutch ovens will help distribute heat around the oven. You can start with a low to moderate heat and then build it up as you need more heat. Remember, you can open up your Dutch oven and watch what is happening inside. If you need to change the amount of heat up or down, do so. Just take off some coals or add some, whichever the case may be. But do not let down on the job. Keep an eye on what you are cooking.

If you are going to cook with wood, use whatever wood you may have. You will probably want to have one main fire and a small area where you will cook. You will be able to bring some coals to the cooking area with your shovel. Be sure you start your fire at least a half hour before you want to start cooking. This will give you enough time to get an adequate amount of coals. After your fire has been burning for some time, it will burn down to where you mainly have coals at the bottom. At this point, you can cook and should have an ample supply of coals.

One point of safety: If you are burning commercially made wood products, be careful not to inhale the fumes. The wood products may have a substance known as Chromate-Copper-Arsenate (CCA). This was used in some manufacturing and will give off a poisonous gas when burnt.

If you choose to use charcoal briquets as I do, you will find that you will have better control of the heat on your oven. I always use charcoal briquets whenever I can. You don't have to put up with the smoke from some woods, and it is generally more convenient, and you can have almost absolute control with them. They are also cleaner to use.

I would suggest that you make yourself a coal starting bucket to start your coals, and to hold them while you are cooking. You can make one from a simple gallon can with air holes cut around the bottom, or you can get a 3 - 5 gallon metal bucket (like a paint can), and put a piece of wire mesh about one third of the way up from the bottom. Put some air holes around the bottom and cut one larger hole on the side at the bottom to put papers in to start a fire. You can always start your coals with charcoal starter fluid, which is quite acceptable.

If you go out to cook for a large party or group of friends like a family reunion, you are going to need a large number of coals. You may need more than one bucket for coals or you can even use an old barbecue and make a big pile in it.

In the next chapter I will talk about how many coals to use as a starting point.

Probably the biggest enemy of the Dutch oven cook is Mother Nature, in the form of wind. Wind will effect how hot your coals are during the cooking time. If you get a breeze while you are cooking, you will find that the oven will heat to a higher temperature on the upwind side. So just rotate your oven regularly. One quarter turn will do nicely.

Remember Fire Safety

I have talked about different types of fires for cooking. Fire safety is also a definite must.

If you are cooking outside with briquets, you will want to be careful that all the coals stay in your cooking spot. They are extremely hot and a small child or adult could get burned by them if they were to try to pick one up with their bare hands.

Never take charcoal briquets inside while they are burning. They will give off a toxic gas which can kill in a confined area. If it starts to rain while you are cooking, just put up a tarp or umbrella. I have had to do this many times when cooking with friends for large groups.

There are some great tools available to help in your cooking, as I have mentioned earlier. Use lid lifters to handle hot lids and ovens. And be sure to use tongs and shovels to handle the hot coals.

Always be careful when you are cooking. Remember that most shoes are now made of synthetic materials, most of which will melt. Many of the materials that clothes are made of today will also burn easily, so keep them from touching the hot coals or the burning fire.

Remember, you can prevent most accidents if you will just think about what you are doing and have the proper respect for the fires and hot ovens.

Outdoor kitchens can be made in a variety of ways. Above is a wooden cabinet style with breadboard and towel rack. Below is a portable kitchen using a suitcase designed by a cook.

Chapter 2

Cooking With Your Dutch Oven

"NOTES"

We have talked about the tools, fires and safety, now we need to get you cooking in your dutch oven.

No matter if you are in your back yard, or in the mountains, you will have best results if you will be sure to level your oven. I find it handy to carry a small block level in my tools. This is especially true when you start stacking ovens during cooking. If you don't have a level, just pour a little cooking oil in the bottom of the pan and you will be able to level it just fine.

I would suggest that you learn right from the start, that for the best results in any cooking, you should use the best ingredients. That's real butter, not margarine, best quality meat, not bargain cuts, fresh vegetables not canned, and so on. If you want to get the best food out of your Dutch oven, be sure to put in the best ingredients.

When you find a recipe you like, don't be afraid to modify it. That's the way new recipes come about. If you have a larger group than the recipe calls for, just adjust the quantities and the size of the oven to accommodate your group. Above all, don't be afraid to try things. That is how we all learn. And never be afraid to ask questions. Remember, there is no such thing as a dumb question.

Altitude Can Make a Difference

When you go into the mountains and start to cook a meal, you will want to adjust your times. As you go to higher altitudes, the cooking times will increase taking longer than if you were at a lower altitude.

If you try to cook specialty dishes like candy or fudge, remember that boiling points are different at different altitudes so use a thermometer.

Utensils Can Make Your Job Easier

I think one of the great things about cooking in modern times, is the large number of gadgets that have been created by inventors to help make our job easier and to give the devout cook some new toys to play with.

Seriously though, there are many great aids to cooking. Metal cake cooling racks can be used as meat racks in the bottom of your oven (or you can also use vegetables or bones to keep your meat off the bottom). Canning lids will work well for holding cornish game hens off the bottom of the oven. You can use pizza pans, bread pans cake pans, pie tins and even pyrex bowls to cook in your oven. Just put some even flat rocks in the bottom of the oven to set them on. That will allow the hot air to circulate around the pans.

One of the best modern day inventions that will save you hours in the long run is aluminum foil. It is not only helpful in cooking but will help you many times in cleaning up after cooking. I like to line my oven with extra heavy duty foil when making cobblers, upside-down cakes and many other dishes with a sugar sauce or such. You can even lift a cake out of the oven and put it on a plate to turn it over, which will make it so you don't have to handle a hot oven. Another use is to make a small bowl out of foil which you can put in the bottom of an oven to mix up sauces. Then just throw it away when you are finished.

Anyone that knows me well, knows that I believe that if you are going to serve your friends food, I like to make it look its best. Garnish every dish appropriately. You can use fresh herbs or fruit or vegetables, but please make it look good. For some reason it will taste better if you do.

Some Helpful Hints

When you are cooking breads and rolls, you can speed up the rising time by putting 3 - 4 briquets on the lid of your oven where you are letting the dough rise. This will give you just the right amount of heat.

I would like to give you a starting point for judging the proper heat in your oven. If you are cooking with a 14 inch oven, start out with about 16 - 18 coals on the bottom for frying or roasting, and 12 on the lid. If you are baking (325-350 F.) bread, rolls or cakes, put only 6 -8 on the bottom of a 14 inch oven and 16 -18 on the top. You will notice that there is quite a difference. You will have to watch your food as you cook even after you get good at deciding the number of coals you will cook with. Just adjust the numbers according to the type of cooking you are doing.

This is an area where again you will probably hear different ideas from each cook, but this is what I have found to work well for me.

When you are planning the shopping list for many items it is helpful to have some guidelines to follow. Here are a few:

Potatoes...1 per person

Beef...6 - 8 oz. per person

Chicken...2 1/2 pieces per person

Ribs...3 per person

Soups...8 oz. per person

Stews...8 - 12 oz. per person.

Cobblers...6 oz. serving per person

These figures are only intended to give you a starting point. You will, over time, develop your own shopping guidelines. Use and trust in yourself.

Whatever you cook, feel free to try new ideas and new recipes and by all means, Bon Appetit!

A small garden rake doubles as a lifting tool and works quite well for smaller ovens.

Custom made tables to cook on can be made to meet your own specifications. Be sure the steel top is at least 3/16" plate steel or thicker. This will keep it from buckling.

Part 2

Cooking in The Dutch Oven

This handy utensil carrier will store all of the needed utensils, and rolls up and ties to keep them all stored intact.

Most dishes you cook at home can be prepared in a Dutch oven outdoors, with equally tasty results.

Chapter 3

On The Simple Side

"NOTES"

_____

_____

_____

_____

_____

_____

_____

_____

_____

_____

_____

_____

_____

_____

_____

_____

_____

_____

_____

_____

When entertaining, we want to make our guest feel special. This is also good for your family. There are a lot of natural items to choose from:

A milk pitcher filled with wild flowers.

A straw basket filled with vine-ripened cherry tomatoes.

Napkins folded around flowers from your garden.

Make an edible centerpiece of peas, peppers, carrots, and tomatoes, etc.

A vase filled with mint sprigs.

Pot roast

1 beef roast (allow 1/2 lb per person)
1/3 cup vegetable oil
salt and pepper to taste
onion salt
celery salt
onions, chunked
green peppers, chunked
1 potato per person
1/2 carrot per person
1 large can mushroom slices
1/2 cup beef broth

Heat oil in oven. When hot, brown roast on all sides. Turn to keep juices in. Drain off fat. Season to taste. Pour in beef broth. Put lid on and cook at 325 F. for 1 1/2 to 2 1/2 hours, depending on the size of your roast. Add vegetables after meat has cooked 45-60 minutes (or about 1/2 hour before you think your meat will be ready). Continue cooking until vegetables are nice and tender. Spoon pan juices over meat and vegetables during cooking.

Hint: This same cooking technique can be used for pork roasts. If you desire gravy with your meat, reserve pan juices after removing meat and vegetables and add a cornstarch mixture or roux, to thicken.

Chicken Livers

1 lb. chicken livers
flour
salt and pepper to taste
4 eggs, beaten
oil, to cook in bottom of oven

Dip livers in egg mixture and then into flour. Put directly into Dutch oven that has been heated and oil is hot. Fry, turning until done.

Barbecued Beef

3 lbs ground beef
3 large onions, chopped
salt and pepper to taste
2 T. flour

Brown meat, and saute onions and seasonings. Sprinkle flour over meat and stir before adding sauce.

Sauce:
1 pint catsup
1 pint water
2 t. curry powder
2 bay leaves
2 T. Worcestershire sauce

Mix all ingredients and boil together. Add meat mixture and simmer for 1 1/2 hours. Serve on buns.

ONIONS

The family of onions, from chives, scallions, leeks, and shallots to the many varieties of the basic onion - Spanish, Italian, Bermuda, Walla Walla, Vidalia, Maui, pearl, Ebenezer, and globe - form a tear-inspiring array. But can you imagine cooking without them?

EGGS BY THE DOZEN

SCRAMBLE WITH-
Chives & cottage cheese, Smoked salmon & dill, parmesan cheese, sauteed onions, minced sun-dried tomatoes & peppers, cheddar cheese & a dab of Sour cream and top with black olives.

POACH WITH-
English muffins, & Canadian bacon or tomato slices, Cornbread with mushrooms & cream sauce, or avacado slices & salsa.

Mock Cheese and Sausage Souffle

1/2 to 1 lb. cooked sausage
1/2 to 1 lb. cheddar cheese
20 eggs, beaten
3/4 cup milk
12-15 slices bread
1 t. mustard powder
Butter

Cook sausage or use pre-cooked. Butter slices of bread. Cut off crusts. Cube bread slices and put in bottom of well greased 12" Dutch oven. Beat eggs well adding milk until blended. Add mustard powder, blend. Shred cheese. Scatter cheese over bread in Dutch oven. Pour egg mixture over cheese. Scatter sausage over top of egg mixture. Cook about 300 F. for 30-40 minutes. Use 5-6 coals bottom, 10-12 coals top.

Steak Stack'n

1 - 1 1/2 lbs round steak
2 T. bacon grease
8 strips bacon, cooked crisp, crumbled
2-3 medium potatoes, shredded
4-5 medium carrots, shredded
4 sweet onions, sliced

2 sweet bell peppers, sliced
1/2 cup water
flour
salt and pepper to taste

Cut round steak into quite large individual servings. Pound in as much flour on both sides as possible. Cook bacon first, until crisp, leaving bacon grease in bottom of Dutch oven. Brown steaks on one side until nicely brown in bottom of Dutch oven with bacon grease. Turn browned side up and quickly brown on other side. While meat is cooking, place a mound of each vegetable on top of each steak piece, with peppers and onions on top. Salt and pepper between layers if desired. Pour in water, cover and simmer. Steam until vegetables are tender. When done, remove each steak intact with vegetables.

TABLESPOONS AND OUNCES

1 pinch=less than 1/8 teaspoon (dry)
1 dash=3 drops to 1/4 teaspoon (liquid)
3 teaspoons (t.) =1 tablespoon (T.)
    = 1/2oz.
2 tablespoons=1 oz.
4 tablespoons=2 oz.=1/4 cup
8 tablespoons=4 oz.=1/2 cup (1 stick of
    butter)
8 tablespoons (flour)=about 2 oz.
16 tablespoons=8 oz.=1 cup=1/2 pound
32 tablespoons=16 oz.=2 cups=1 pound
64 tablespoons=32 oz.=1 quart=2 pounds

"Red skies in morning Sailors take warning Red skies at night Sailors delight."

CHIVES

This mild and sweet onion is easy to grow indoors and out. It is best when snipped into irregular pieces and scattered over a dish at the last moment. You can keep a pot growing by a sunny window year round and you can use the pretty lavender blossoms as a garnish also.

Vera's Baked Beans

1/2 lb bacon
1 lb lean ground beef
1 large onion
1 small green pepper
1/2 cup brown sugar
1/2 cup catsup
16 oz. homestyle chili sauce
2 T. mustard
1/2 lb. pre-cooked ham, cubed
2 31oz. cans pork and beans

Brown bacon and ground beef in 12" Dutch oven, preheated over 9-10 coals. Chop onion and green pepper and saute with meat until tender. Drain off excess fat. Add brown sugar, catsup, chili sauce, and mustard. Simmer for 15 minutes. Add beans and ham. Cover and add approximately 15 coals to lid. Simmer for 2 hours.

This recipe has been handed down by Vera Sorensen of Manti, Utah and it is loved by everyone who has tried it. You'll love it too!

Dutch Oven Sloppy Joes

4 lbs. lean ground beef
2 med. onions
1 bell pepper

2 12oz. cans tomato paste
4 pkg. Schilling sloppy Joe seasoning mix

topping:

4 cups bisquick
1 1/3 cups water

Put ground beef, chopped onions
and peppers in 14" Dutch oven.
Brown ground beef and saute peppers and onion until clear.   Add
tomato paste, water and seasoning
mix. Cover and bring to a simmer.
Mix bisquick and water until soft
dough forms. Drop by spoonfuls
onto simmering sloppy joe mix.
Bake to golden brown or until an
inserted toothpick comes out clean.
Use 10-12 coals on bottom and 16-
18 on top. Serves 10-15.

Navajo Tacos

Use your favorite bread recipe
or frozen ready to bake rolls
chili, homemade or canned
onions, diced
lettuce,chopped or sliced
green onions, chopped
peppers, diced,
cheese, shredded
taco sauce
sour cream

**EXPERI-
MENT ON
YOUR OWN**

If you like cook-
ing, you want to
learn about it
through taste,
feel, smell and
sight. Taste new
raw ingredients,
spices, herbs, and
flavors before
you add them,
and then after-
ward to see their
effect.

Choose what you will use for your bread. Stretch and pull until dough in very thin and round. Heat oil in Dutch oven. When hot enough, put dough in to fry. About 18-20 coals bottom. Use 12" or 14" Dutch oven. Brown both sides nicely. Remove and let drain on paper towels. Top with chili, lettuce, onions, green peppers, cheese, taco sauce, and if you like, sour cream. Be creative.

Hint: You can also make wonderful scones this way, and top with butter and jam, or honey.

Meat Loaf With Rice

2 lb. ground beef
1/2 lb. pork sausage
2 t. salt
2 t. sugar
1/2 t. ground sage
1/2 t. pepper
4 eggs, well beaten
2 cups cooked rice
2 cups mashed potatoes
2 onions, diced

Mix meat with seasonings and then rest of ingredients. Mix thoroughly. Pat into lightly greased 12" Dutch oven. Bake at 375 F. until done, about 1 to 1 1/2 hours.

MUSHROOMS

They are great raw, marinated or cooked. When stuffed, it becomes a perfect finger food. It is attractive and completely self-contained.

Serves 12-15. Use 8 coals bottom and 18-20 coals top.

Hint: You can also use bacon on this meatloaf the same as the other one if you would like.

"You never get a second chance to make a first impression."
-Will Rogers

Dutch Oven Potatoes and Onions

1 lb. bacon cut in 1 inch pieces
14 potatoes
5 onions
1/4 cup bacon grease (from cooking bacon)
1 cup water

Peel and slice potatoes in 1/4 inch slices. Set aside. Cut up bacon in 1 inch pieces and fry in bottom of 14" Dutch oven. Add potatoes and onions and stir to coat with the bacon grease. Pour in water and season. Bake for about 1 hour at 350 F. Use about 14 coals on the bottom and 6 -8 on the top. Check regularly and stir carefully if needed every 20 minutes.

Hint: You can add in 2 cups mild cheddar cheese and 1/2 cup green onions for the last 20 minutes. This gives it an entirely different taste that will melt in your mouth.

Chapter 4

Meats, Poultry, Fish

"NOTES"

Apple-Raisin Stuffed Chicken Breasts

6-8 boneless chicken breasts
1 boxed stuffing mix or use your favorite recipe
1/2 apple, diced
1/2 cup raisins, boiled
1 cup chicken broth
1/4 cup honey
sweet & sour sauce
corn husks, or grape leaves to wrap around chicken

Mix chicken broth and honey together. Pour over chicken breasts and marinate overnight. Prepare stuffing. Add raisins and apples to stuffing. Put stuffing in middle of chicken breast and roll up into grape leaves or corn husks. Tie with string to hold together. When all are done, heat oven, and cover bottom with a little oil. In 12" Dutch oven use 14-16 coals, as soon as it is hot put in chicken. Turn regularly to cook on all sides. The grape leaves or corn husks, help keep juices intact. Cook for about 20 minutes or until done. Remove grape leaves (if you wish, you can also eat these) or corn husks. Have sweet and sour sauce prepared. Put over chicken. Serve.

Hint: We have often served this

dish in pineapple halves, that have been hollowed out. You can add the pineapple to your sweet and sour sauce, or add it to a fruit pizza, or just enjoy it plain. Arrange chicken in pineapple and then pour the sauce over the top. You can also vary this by changing the stuffing mixture. Try orange-apple, cranberry-orange, etc. You can have a vegetable stuffing and have a cheese or creamed sauce on the top of the chicken. Think of the combinations you like and try them. You don't have to marinate the chicken breasts, but this does add a little different flavor to the meat.

Baked Haddock Fillets

2 lb. frozen haddock fillets, partially thawed
2 t. salt
2 T. melted butter
1 egg yolk, slightly beaten
ground pepper to taste
4 T. fine dry bread crumbs
4 T. freshly grated Parmesan cheese
3/4 cup whipping cream
2 T. chopped dill
1 lb. small cooked shrimp
1 1/2 cups sliced fresh mushrooms

Cut each haddock fillet lengthwise,

COOKING FISH

Many people overcook fish. Lay the fish on its side and measure it with a ruler at its thickest part. You calculate 10 minutes of cooking time, whatever the method, per inch of thickness.

QUICHES

Quiches are easy to prepare and a lot of fun to serve and eat. You can make your crusts from scratch or use frozen. Both work well. For a quiche prepared in a 10"oven, line the bottom with a crust, and cook for about 10 minutes. Add about 3 cups of filling like onions, bacon, mozzarella and olives; or crab, green peppers, and cheddar; or sausage, spinach and parmesan. Beat 4 eggs and add to 1 2/3 cup cream and season to taste. Pour over filling. Sprinkle cheese on top and cook for15-20 minutes more or until egg mixture filling is firm.

to make uniform size fillets. Sprinkle with salt. Melt butter, then add egg yolk and pepper. Brush fillets with half the mixture. Combine bread crumbs and cheese in a bowl. Place buttered side of fish in bread crumb mixture. Place this side down in the bottom of a lightly buttered 12" or 14" Dutch oven. Brush remaining butter-egg mixture on top of fillets. Sprinkle remaining crumb mixture on top. Bake for 15-20 minutes at 425 F. Use 8-10 coals bottom and 16-18 coals top if using 12" oven and 12-16 coals bottom and 18-20 coals top for 14" oven. While it is baking, use foil and make a little bowl. Add cream to foil and bring to boil on the coals on the lid, then remove from heat and add dill. Lift lid and pour cream around haddock fillets. Bake for about 10 more minutes. Add sliced mushrooms and shrimp and heat through. Serves 8-10.

Barbecued Chicken

4 chickens, cut up
4 onions, diced
2 1/2 cups brown sugar
3 1/2 cups water
8 1/2 cups catsup
1 t. tobasco sauce

In 14" or 16" Dutch oven, saute onions until clear. Add all ingredients, except chicken. Mix well. Add chicken and bring to simmer, cooking 1 to 1 1/2 hours or until chicken in tender. Leave lid ajar to let steam out. The sauce will cook down and become thicker.

Hint: You can also use this great recipe for beef and pork ribs. They have to cook longer, but tastes great. You can cook all three together, by starting with pork ribs, letting them cook for 1 hour and then add beef ribs, and cook for 1/2 hour and then add chicken and let cook for 1 hour.

Beef or Pork Stir-fry

4 T. Cornstarch
4 T. Soy Sauce
2 lb. boneless beef sirloin or pork tenderloin
3/4 cup vegetable oil
2 large cloves garlic, minced
4 t. minced ginger root
8 cups vegetables, cut up, use what ever combination you like
  tomatoes
  mushrooms
  bean sprouts
  cauliflower
  celery
  Chinese cabbage

LEMONS

Lemons are great for flavoring and garnishes. The best flavor is usually found in the small, round or oval lemons with smooth skins. Store them at room temperature and you will get more juice from them. You can squeeze juice over an oven of steamed vegetables, or add it to the butter and pour over them. It is good in many soup dishes and helps intensify the flavors. Use lemon juice on cut up fruit to keep it from turning brown.

TYPES OF CHICKEN

Broilers-
1-2 lbs. They are young chickens and have little fat.

Fryers-
2-4 lbs. They will have some yellow fat and plump breasts. You can either broil or fry these, if you prepare them well.

Roasters-
3-7 lbs. They are bred for tenderness and are very meaty. They are great for roasting, baking, & barbecuing.

green onions
green or red bell peppers
onion
pea pods
yellow crookneck squash
zucchini
3 cups chicken or beef broth
8 servings rice or chinese noodles

Slice meat in strips 1/4 inch thick, 2 inches long and 1/2 inch wide. Mix cornstarch and soy sauce together until smooth. Set aside. In Dutch oven, heat 1/2 of oil, and add garlic and ginger root. When hot, add meat, stirring constantly until done. Remove. Add rest of oil. Add vegetables, starting with longest-cooking ones first. Stir and toss constantly. When almost done, return meat to skillet. Add broth and then stir in soy sauce mixture. Let cook a few minutes to thicken, then serve over rice or chinese noodles.

Chicken Pot Pie

3 cups flour
1/2 t. salt
1 cup shortening or lard
2 T. Butter
7-8 T. cold water

Cook filling first and let oven cool

down or have two ovens to use. Cut in shortening or lard and butter with flour and salt. Use pastry blender or 2 knives. Cut in until most pieces are size of peas. Sprinkle cold water evenly over surface, 1 T. at a time, mixing and tossing with fork until flour is moistened. Shape dough into ball, dividing into 1/3 and 2/3. Use the 2/3 ball and roll out between wax paper. Line 12" Dutch oven on bottom and up sides with dough. Put in filling. Roll out top crust. Place on top. Flute edges. Brush crust with egg water mixture and puncture holes in top for steam to escape. Bake at 425 F. for 30 to 35 minutes or until crust is golden brown. Use 8-10 coals bottom and 18-20 coals top.

Filling:

1/2 cup butter
1/2 cup shredded carrot
1/2 cup finely chopped celery
1/2 cups chopped green onion
1/2 cup flour
1 T. Celery salt
2 cups chicken broth
2 cups milk
4 cups cooked chicken or turkey
2 oz. drained sliced mushrooms
1/2 cup chopped pimento
2 cups cooked vegetables
  green beans
  peas

DILL

Dill was discovered in 1597. Since its reeds were used to soothe babies to sleep, its name is taken from the Saxon "dillan," meaning to lull. Dill is a great seasoning with many potato dishes.

potatoes
cauliflower, etc.
1 t. dried rubbed sage
1 t. dried leaf marjoram

Melt butter in oven, adding carrot, celery and green onion. Cook until tender. Stir in flour and celery salt until smooth. Whisk in chicken broth and milk. Cook until thickened, whisking constantly. Stir in chicken or turkey, mushrooms and pimento and cooked vegetables and seasonings. Put into bottom crust in Dutch oven or remove and reserve until oven is cool enough to put crust in.

Cornish Game Hens

Use as many hens as you have people to serve and use your favorite dressing recipe.

See Game Hens with Herb Stuffing in Old Deseret Chapter for basic directions.

Hints: You can vary this dish in many ways. By using different stuffing recipes, like apples and oranges, in the stuffing, raisins, and then basting the hens with an orange glaze made of orange juice, and Karo syrup. You can put currents in the dressing and baste the

SCALLIONS

Scallions are young onions. Depending on the variety, they can be mild or strong. They add color, flavor and crunch to soups and salads and can be used as a garnish.

hens with a raspberry sauce made up of raspberry pancake syrup and Karo syrup and boiling it down. These are excellent ways to vary this dish. Because hens are steamed, you can add vegetables toward the end of the cooking time and have your meal done together.

Crown Roast of Pork

1 10-12 lb. rib Crown roast of pork
1 recipe stuffing
spiced crab apples
Parsley or watercress sprigs

Have butcher prepare crown. Let roast stand at room temperature for 1-2 hours. Place roast in Dutch oven on rack. Place a ball of foil or cooking paper in the center and cover rib ends with foil or bacon. Insert a meat thermometer between two ribs in center of meat, making sure it doesn't touch bones. Roast for 1 1/2 hours with moderate heat. Remove foil from center and fill with stuffing. Loosely cover with foil and roast 1 hour. Remove all foil and continue cooking 15-20 minutes longer. Thermometer should register 170 degrees. Remove coals and let rest 15-20 minutes. This will let the meat firm up. Garnish with apples and parsley or cress. We

THERMOMETERS

There are instant-read thermometers, and these do not remain in the food as it cooks. You merely insert it when you feel it is appropriate and you get and instant reading, & then it is removed. These thermometers are usually more expensive, but they are very accurate and they last longer.

reccomend using a deep 15" or deep 17" oven. Use 10-15 coals bottom, 20-25 coals top.

Stuffing:
1/2 cup minced yellow onion
3/4 cup minced celery and leaves
1/2 cup butter
1 1 /2 qt. bread cubes
1 t. poultry seasoning
1 1 /2 t. salt
1/2 t. pepper
1/4 cup minced parsley
3 cups coarsely chopped apples
3/4 cup seedless white raisins
1/2 cup apple sauce or juice

Saute onion and celery in butter five minutes or until pale golden. Mix with remaining ingredients, tossing with two forks. Place slice of bread in center of crown before filling to prevent stuffing from falling through the rack. Proceed as instructed above.

Firehouse Chili

6 lb. cubed beef
1/2 cup butter
5 large onions, diced
4 green bell peppers, diced
4 cloves garlic, minced
2-3 bay leaves
3 T. chili powder
1 T. paprika

DRIED PEAS & BEANS

Rinse them through a strainer under cold running water and sort to remove any pebbles or other objects you may find. Sometimes it is beneficial to the recipe to soak them overnight. Cover them by 3-4 inches. They will absorb quite a lot of water. Some favorites are black-eyes peas, garbanzos or chick-peas, kidney beans, lentils, lima beans, pinto beans, red beans, soybeans, split peas and white beans.

6 cups tomato sauce
3 T. bouillon in
2/3 cup red wine vinegar
2 T. tobasco sauce
1 T. oregano
2 cans diced green chillies (7 oz)
1 1/2 T. cumin
Season to taste

Heat oven over 8-10 coals. Melt butter and add meat in 14" oven. Cook until all the meat is brown. Add onions and bell peppers. Saute until tender. Add all of the other ingredients. Mix well. Cover and simmer for 2-3 hours (you will need to watch your coals and add more as needed) until meat melts in your mouth. On this recipe, you can add or subtract the tobasco sauce for a milder or hotter dish.

Islander Fish Roll-ups w/Pina Colada Butter

6-8 fillets of white fish (orange roughy)
Pina Colada Butter
3 carrots, cut in strips
6-8 Broccoli Spears

Steam carrots and broccoli until desired tenderness, leaving crisp enough to saute a few minutes in pina colada butter. Wrap fillets around carrots and broccoli. Tie

HANDLING HOT PEPPERS

When handling hot peppers you need to do so with care. The seeds are what contain the fire, and whenever you handle peppers, be sure to wash your hands good before you touch your mouth or rub your eyes.

FROM THE CHEF'S NOTEBOOK

If you want to try something different when the recipe calls for Cornish game hens, try substituting the plump meaty little chickens called Poussins. They are fed a natural blend of corn, barley, and soy and allowed free range. They are killed at the age of three weeks and hand-dressed.

roll-ups with string. Cook fish turning as needed until done. Baste with pina colada butter. Serve. Make pina colada butter by whipping cream of coconut & pineapple juice with butter. You can make it strong or mild, depending on your own tastes. To cook the fish, you are using bottom heat mostly. Use 12" oven with 10-12 coals on the bottom. Serves 6-8.

Meat Loaf with Bread

2 lb ground beef
2 lb. ground pork sausage
6 eggs, beaten
2 t. salt
1 t. pepper
2 1/2 cups whole milk
4 cups bread or cracker crumbs
2 large onions, diced
1/2 cup catsup
1 1b. bacon

Combine all ingredients in bowl except bacon. Mix very well. Line 12"Dutch oven with 1/2 of bacon. Pat meatloaf on top of bacon very firmly. Place other 1/2 half of bacon on top of meat loaf. Bake for 1 1/2 to 2 hours at 350 F. Use 8 coals bottom and 16-18 coals top. Serves 12-15.

Hint: Stuffed green bell peppers

PEPPER

Called the "spice of life," it was once only available to the rich. Now it is hard to imagine cooking without it. New peppers have become available for our use. White pepper, is dried, pink and green come packed in water or vinegar. Invest in a good peppermill, as ground black pepper loses its vitality soon after it is ground.

are a favorite with many people. Use this meatloaf recipe to stuff the peppers. Put in Dutch oven and cover with tomato sauce made up of stewed tomatoes, onions, celery and a little chili powder and garlic salt. Cook 45-60 minutes on medium heat. Coals same as meat loaf. It is also great to use for stuffed cabbage. Bring water to a boil in your oven, and add cabbage leaves until they are tender enough to roll up. Cut the big vein at the base of the cabbage leaf off to the same depth as the rest of the leaf. Add meat at the bottom of the leaf and roll up. Tuck ends of cabbage into the middle of the rolls. Put in oven and cover with similar sauce (or another favorite of your choice) as the peppers and proceed the same.

Pineapple Up-side-down Ham Loaf

3 eggs
3/4 cup milk
1 1/2 T. prepared mustard
1/8 t. ground cloves
1 1/4 lb ground cooked ham
1 cup fine cracker crumbs
6 T. Brown sugar
10-12 pineapple slices
6 maraschino cherries, halved
1/8 t. ground nutmeg

PINEAPPLE

Known as a symbol of hospitality, the English at one time rented them for centerpieces. Look for the ripest ones you can find. Touch for tenderness, and smell for sweetness. Watch the color. Choose the ones with a golden hue. Once they have been picked they will no longer increase in sweetness, but they will get softer.

FROM THE CHEF'S NOTEBOOK

If you don't want to go to the trouble of an up-side-down loaf, put the meat mixture in the bottom of the oven and spoon a glaze of pineapple ice-cream topping, cinnamon and nutmeg over the top of the loaf.

3/4 lb lean ground pork sausage
3 T. melted butter

Blend eggs, milk, crackers, spices, ham, sausage, mustard in food processor for a few minutes until well mixed, or by hand for 10-15 minutes. Combine melted butter and brown sugar in bottom of 12" oven. Arrange pineapple slices and cherries into desired pattern on top of butter-sugar mixture. Pat ham mixture onto pineapple. Bake for 45-60 minutes, at about 300 F. Use 6-8 coals bottom and 10-12 top. Pour off excess juices and fat. Invert, and serve.

Hint: We like to use foil to line the oven, although this isn't necessary, it does make clean-up easier, and turning the ham loaf is easier in the foil, than the Dutch oven. You can take the ham loaf out of the dutch oven, let one side of the foil down, to drain off excess juices, and then turn it onto serving platter.

HAM BALLS

If you would like, use the Ham Loaf recipe to make ham balls. Spoon drops of the mixture in the bottom of the oven and bake like meatballs. The ham balls are excellent served over noodles and topped with a cream sauce.

Primed With Bacon

1 5 lb.or larger standing rib roast
or prime rib
1 lb. bacon
layer of fat

Choose an oven appropriate to the size of roast you are cooking or vice versa. You can do up to a 24 lb. full prime rib in a 22" Dutch oven. A 15 - 18 lb. rib shuld fit in a 17" oven and an 8 - 12 lb. rib should fit in a 15" oven. Lay strips of bacon on top of roast, cover with fat. Let stand at room temperature for 1 1/2 - 2 hours. Place on rib bones arranged in bottom of deep Dutch oven, fat side up. Bones act as rack, or use conventional cooking rack instead. Place over low heat. Insert meat thermometer in middle of roast, avoiding bones, and roast to desired temperature. Remove from heat, let stand 10-15 minutes before slicing. Serve with Horseradish sauce.

Hint: Roasts with fewer than five ribs may not be as moist. The following is a chart to help you determine how you would like your roast cooked.

Rare	120-125 F.
Medium rare	130-140 F.
Medium	145-150 F.
Well done	155-160 F.

FROM THE CHEF'S NOTEBOOK

Entertaining and sharing meals should be as natural and sincere as anything else you do. You don't have to be formal or organized to put over your personal style and feelings. It is important to bring together the people you care about, to share food and have a great time together.

Ranchero Chili

2 lb. ground beef or pork sausage, or 1 lb. of each
1 1/2 cups onions, diced
1 1/2 cups green bell peppers, diced
1 32 oz. can stewed tomatoes
1 16 oz. can tomato sauce
1 can whole kernel corn
5 T. Worcestershire sauce
3 t. oregano
4 t. chili powder
1 t. tabasco sauce
32 oz. canned red beans, drained, rinsed (may be omitted if desired)

In 12" oven, add meat, onions, and bell peppers. Cook using 12-16 coals, until meat is brown and vegetables partially cooked. Add everything else. Bring to a boil, and then simmer about 45 minutes until everything is tender and flavors blend. Stir occasionally.

Hint: This is a great chili and works great with the Navajo Tacos recipe. If eating just the chili, try adding crackers, diced chilies, shredded cheese and diced white or yellow onion, or green onion as a topping in your bowl.

Roast Turkey

1 turkey

CHILI POWDER

Chili powders found on most supermarket shelves have been blended from many spices and herbs that produce a rather bland seasoning. It is becoming easier to find individual powdered chiles without the other added ingredients. There is very little loss of flavor in these dried powders and are a great substitute for the peppers themselves.

stuffing of your choice
butter basting sauce or glaze if preferred

Choose size of turkey desired. Make your favorite stuffing. Rinse turkey. Pat turkey dry. Twist wings behind. Stuff. Depending on size of turkey, you may be using a deep 15", 17" or 22" Dutch oven. Place roasting rack in bottom of oven. Place turkey on top of rack. Baste with desired sauce. Cooking times are approximately as follows: 8-12 lbs., 3-4 hours, 12-16 lbs., 3 1/2 to 5 hours, 16-20 lbs., 4 1/2 to 6 hours, 20-24 lbs., 5 1/2-6 1/2 hours.

Butter Basting Sauce
1/2 cup butter
2 t. dried leaf herbs
1/2 t. celery salt
1/2 t. onion salt

Heat butter until melted. Stir in herbs, celery and onion salts. Mix well. Stir before brushing on poultry.

Cranberry Glaze
1/2 cup cranberry-orange relish
1/2 cup orange marmalade
2 T. orange liqueur or orange juice
1/2 t. all-spice

In bowl, mix together relish,

TIPS ABOUT ROASTING

Place bird on rack so it does not stew in its own juice. Unstuffed birds cook more quickly than stuffed birds. Meaty birds cook more slowly than bony birds. Refrigerated birds cook more slowly than birds at room temperature.

preserves, liqueur or fruit juice and spice. Mix well. Baste during last 1/2 hour of cooking time on poultry.

Hints: There are many combinations of glazes. Cranberry-apricot with apricot brandy or apricot nectar and cardamom for spice, Cranberry-pineapple using pineapple preserves with cranberry juice cocktail and ginger for spice. Be creative and try alternatives.

Smothered Chicken

6 chicken breasts(either with or w/o bone)
4 cups rice (cooked)
2 small cans sliced mushrooms
1 small bottle chopped pimentos
1 qt. chicken stock
1 cup cream
1 cup slivered almonds
1/2 cup flour
cayenne pepper
1 t. lemon juice
salt to taste
Oil

CUBING CHICKEN

Chicken is easier to cut into cubes after chilling because cubes retain their shape better. A one-pound whole chicken breast yields about 1 cup chicken cubes. A three-pound whole chicken yields about 2 cups chicken cubes.

In 14" Dutch oven, cover bottom with oil. Cook chicken until almost done. Remove and set aside. Make sauce in the dutch oven using chicken stock, cream and flour. Pour liquid from mushrooms into sauce. Mix in mushrooms, pimentos, almonds, seasonings and lemon juice. Add rice into sauce. Add chicken back to rice mixture. Put lid on oven and bake for about 45 minutes at 325 F. Use 6-8 coals bottom, 14-16 coals top.

Spanish Style Chicken

2 chickens, cut up
oil
10 tomatoes, diced
2 green, red or yellow bell peppers, diced
2 yellow or white onions, diced
2 cloves garlic,chopped
1 cup sliced mushrooms (or buttons if you like)
1 chili pepper, diced (we like mild, but you choose what you like)
1/2 cup sweet wine
Salt and pepper to taste
garlic salt
celery salt

Heat oil in bottom of 14" Dutch oven. When hot, brown chicken. Remove. Saute vegetables (except tomatoes and mushrooms) Remove. Arrange chicken, so as to cover the bottom. Add all vegetables and season to taste. Let simmer 30-40 minutes or until done. You can serve this plain or with rice or noodles. What ever you like.

FROM THE CHEF'S NOTEBOOK

A picnic does not need to be lunch in the park. It can be anywhere and just about anytime. It is usually eating in the open with friends or family. It can be for breakfast, lunch or dinner or even a sunset feast. Most items eaten outdoors taste wonderful. Most of the foods you like to fix at home can be accommodated to the out of doors. Just use your imagination.

Stuffed Beef Tenderloin

1 3 lb. beef tenderloin, butterflied
1/4 cup finely chopped onion
3 T. butter, softened
1/4 lb. bread, dried
1/4 cup cooked sausage
1/4 cup roasted pinenuts
1/4 cup finely chopped celery
1 t. dried leaf herbs
4 T. beef broth
3 T. butter, softened
3/4 t. pepper
3/4 t. garlic salt

Cook sausage, adding onions, celery and pinenuts, to saute. Crumble bread, and add seasonings. Combine with vegetables and sausage mixture. Add 3 T. butter and mix in. Add only enough beef broth to moisten. Lay out tenderloin. Place stuffing in the middle. Roll up, tieing to keep together. Keep as much stuffing in as possible. Blend together 3 T. butter, 3/4 t. pepper and 3/4 t. garlic salt. Blend well. Spread butter mixture over tenderloin before cooking. Place in 12" Dutch oven. Use 8 coals bottom and 14-16 coals on top. Cook for about 40-50 minutes. Baste with juices occasionally.

Stuffed Trout or Red Snapper

4 trout or red snapper
1/4 cup shredded monterey jack cheese or cheddar
3 T. chopped parsley
2 cups bread, cubed
1 egg, beaten
2 T. butter
1/4 cup diced onion
1/4 cup chopped celery
1/2 cup cooked baby shrimp

Saute onion and celery in butter. Add to cubed bread. Toss gently. Add parsley, cheese and shrimp. Add egg mixture to moisten. Lightly season inside cavity of fish. Stuff cavity of fish. Lightly brush fish with butter and season to taste. Bake in a 14" Dutch oven, lightly oiled. 10-12 coals on the bottom and 16-18 on top.

Hint: You could also stuff any large fish fillet or steak that can be pocketed.

Swiss Steak Elegante

1 lb. bacon
8 pieces beef round steak
1/2 cups dry white wine

"Fish, to taste right, must swim three times - in water, in butter, and in wine."
-Polish Proverb

2 cups fresh mushrooms, sliced
4 tomatoes, peeled
1/2 cup shallots
1 clove garlic
1/4 cup chopped parsley
1 cup yellow onions, chopped
1 cup green peppers, chopped
1/2 cup carrots, julienne
1 green onion

In bottom of Dutch oven, cook bacon over medium heat until crisp. Remove bacon and drain and set aside. In bottom of oven, brown steaks in bacon drippings. Add wine, onions, peppers, carrots, shallots and tomatoes and bake for 1 1/2 hrs over low heat. Spoon pan juices over meat during cooking. Before serving, remove most of liquid and reserve for gravy if desired. Top with bacon, crumbled, green onion, parsley and serve. Serves 8. Use 12" or 14" oven.

Trail Beans

1 12 oz. pkg. dry red beans
4 cups water
1/4 lb. salt pork, diced
2 lb. beef, cubed
1 cup onions, diced
1 6 oz. can tomato paste
4 t. chili powder
1 t. each salt, cumin seed, crushed dried red pepper

"Those things are better which are perfected by nature than those which are finished by art."
-Cicero

2 bay leaf

Wash beans and soak overnight in cold water, drain. Cook salt pork in 12" oven, add beef and brown. Remove and reserve. Put beans in Dutch oven, add water and simmer 1 hour. Add meat to beans with remaining ingredients. Cover and simmer for two hours, adding hot water as needed. Makes 6-8 servings.

FROM THE CHEF'S NOTEBOOK

When soaking beans, use 8 cups *soaking* water for 1 pound of beans and 6 cups *cooking* water for 1 pound of beans.

This wonderful Crown Roast of Pork (page 62) is an excellent example of a dish you can prepare for your family or a group of friends. It is sure to be a winner!

Chapter 5

Soups, Stews & Sauces

"NOTES"

_____

_____

_____

_____

_____

_____

_____

_____

_____

_____

_____

_____

_____

_____

_____

_____

_____

_____

_____

_____

_____

Barbecue Sauce

2 strips bacon, chopped fine
3 T. minced green bell pepper
1 onion, minced
1 clove garlic, cut fine
1 t. salt
1 t. chili powder
1/2 cup vinegar
1/2 cup packed brown sugar
1 cup tomato juice

Brown bacon. Add green pepper, onion, garlic, and cover with water. Simmer for about 10 minutes. Add remaining ingredients and cook just long enough to blend flavors. About 20-30 minutes. Season to taste. Use as needed.

Cheese Sauce

3 T. Shortening or butter
3 T. flour
2 1/2 cups milk
1/3 lb. cheese, grated
salt and pepper to taste

Melt butter and then blend in flour, cooking until flour taste is gone. Add milk and continue cooking over low heat until thick and smooth. Add cheese and stir until melted.

Cream of Potato Soup

12 potatoes, diced
water to barely cover
2 cups cream
3 onions, chunked
2 chicken bullion cube
1/2 cup chopped parsley
1/2 -2/3 cup roux

Place diced potatoes and onions in 12" or 14" Dutch oven. Add enough water to barely cover. Add 2 chicken bullion cubes, crushed so they will dissolve quickly. Simmer until potatoes and onions are done. Add cream and bring back to simmer. Add roux enough to thicken. Stir in chopped parsley.

Roux

1/2 cup butter
1/2 cup flour

Melt butter over medium heat. Add flour and cook a few minutes. I like to let the flour mixture brown a little, but not burn. This gives a nutty flavor to the roux. Makes about 1/2 cup.

MEMORIES

There is nothing like soup to make you feel secure and warm, recalling the love and care that went into years of your childhood.

SOUP

In the Middle Ages, French peasants, first provided the inspiration for the soup we enjoy today. Because of the lack of eating utensils, they were forced to sop up the stewed meat juices with bread. Their evening meal was known as la soupe.

Fisherman's Clam Chowder

3 6oz cans minced clams
1 1/2 cups finely chopped onion
1 1/2 cups finely diced celery
3 cups finely diced potatoes
3/4 cup butter
3/4 cup flour
1 qt. half & half
1 1/2 t. salt
dash of pepper
2 T. red wine vinegar
1 T. chopped parsley

Drain juice of clams and pour over vegetables. Add enough water to barely cover and simmer covered until potatoes are tender. (Melt butter, add flour, blend and cook a minute or two. This should be done first to make the roux, then add it after the vegetables are cooked, to thicken). Add cream and stir until thick. Add vegetables and clams and seasonings. Heat through. Serves 12-15. Use 12" or 14" Dutch oven.

Horseradish Sauce

1 T. cider vinegar
2 T. Horseradish sauce
1 cup sour cream

Mix well and serve with roast beef.

Mediterranean Lamb Stew

1 lb. cubed lamb
8 cups water
6 cups chopped vegetables
  onion
  green pepper
  sliced green olives
  tomatoes
  zuchinni
4 t. beef-bouillon granules
1 t. mint
1 t. lemon peel
1 bay leaf
4 t. Worcestershire sauce
1 cup quick-cooking brown rice

Combine lamb, water, vegetables, bouillion granules, herbs, bay leaf and Worcestershire sauce. Bring to a boil over high heat. Reduce heat, and simmer 1 1/2 to 2 hours or until meat is tender. Add brown rice. Bring to boil on high heat. Simmer 40 to 45 minutes or until rice is tender. Remove bay leaf. Skim off excess fat.

Hints: You can vary this stew by changing vegetables and seasonings also. Use your favorites.

Mulligan Stew

3 lb. stew meat, beef, pork, lamb

STEW POTS

Stews are a forgiving food. Easygoing and open to substitution. They can reduce pressure in the kitchen, as they can always be prepared ahead a day or two or move in advance of serving. The finished product is always welcome.

cut in 1" cubes
3 cups beef or chicken broth
2 T. vegetable oil
1 28 oz. can tomatoes, cut up
2 t. basil
2 t. oregano
1 large bay leaf
2 T. Worcestershire sauce
9 cups fresh cut up vegetables
  potatoes
  carrots
  onions
  corn
2 cups frozen peas
1 can kidney beans
1/3 cup flour
2/3 cup cold water

SOUP GARNISHES

Sometimes it is a challenge to provide a garnish that offers a complementary contrast in taste, color and texture without overwhelming the soup. Fresh herbs, pasta, grated cheese, fruits, cream, a sprinkling of vegetables, should all complement the flavor already developed, so choose the right combinations.

In 12" Dutch oven, add oil. When hot add meat. Cook about 20 minutes to brown all sides. Drain off fat. Pour broth and tomatoes over meat. Stir in herbs. Add bay leaf and worcestershire sauce. Bring to boil over high heat. Add fresh vegetables. Bring to boil. Reduce and simmer for 20 minutes. Add frozen vegetables, simmer 10 to 15 minutes. Combine flour and water. During last few minutes, add to thicken.

Hints: Instead of tomatoes, bay leaves, basil and oregano, add taco sauce and chili powder. Use pinto beans instead of kidney bean, and for vegetables use green peppers, small corn on the cob pieces, zucchini strips and omit frozen peas. This makes a nice mexican stew. Or if you prefer oriental, substitute canned sweet & sour sauce and broth for the liquid, use ginger for the spice. Use fresh mushroom slices, red-pepper strips, green onions, water chestnuts and thawed frozen pea pods for the vegetables.

White Sauce

1/2 cup butter
1/2 cup flour
1/2 t. salt or flavored salt
pepper
2 cups milk

In oven, melt butter over medium heat, 6-8 coals. Whisk in flour, salt and pepper. Cook for a few minutes. Whisk in milk and cook until thick and bubbly.

Hints: The butter and flour mixture is called roux (pg. 80). You can make this in different quantities, always using equal parts of butter and flour. This is a great thickening agent for soups and gravies. White sauces are very versatile. You can add fresh herbs, cheeses, etc., to compliment many dishes.

SORREL

If you want a tart and lemony flavor, consider using sorrel. It is available in many varieties. When using, you need to add a little at a time and test for the taste you are trying for. It is a great seasoning if you are avoiding using salt. Use a little in coleslaw or other salads, or instead of lettuce on a sandwich, add a handful of chopped sorrel to any potato or cream soup.

CROUTONS

A simple garnish can sometimes be the best. Crisp croutons, made of good-quality bread and that are well toasted or sauteed, can make a soup or stew something special. Cut the bread into 1/2 inch cubes and spread them out on the bottom of the Dutch oven. Bake at 400 F., until crisp and brown. Takes about 10-15 minutes. Or, if you like, saute a little bit of garlic in butter in the Dutch oven, add the bread cubes and saute over medium heat, stirring and tossing the cubes until golden brown. Be sure to set them on a paper towel to absorb before using.

Split Pea Soup

3 cups split peas
4 qts water
1/2 lb bacon, cooked and crumbled
1 onion
1 carrot, shredded
1 cup chopped celery
salt and pepper to taste
6 T. butter
6 T. flour

Melt butter and add flour to make roux. Cook bacon, split peas and water until peas are tender. Add vegetables, cook slowly, add roux to thicken. Cook 15 minutes longer, stirring frequently.

Hints: You can use ground beef or ham for the meat instead of the bacon. Try it different ways. Serve with croutons as garnish.

Stew For The Masses

33 lbs lean ground beef
90 potatoes, diced
10 lbs onions, diced
30 lbs carrots, sliced
15 heads celery
15 heads cauliflower
3 #10 cans corn
2 #10 cans kidney beans
4 40-oz. pkg. frozen peas

6 16-oz. pkg. frozen green beans

Seasonings:
30 bay leaves
1 1/2 cups sugar
2/3 cup salt
3 T. paprika
1 T. allspice
1 1/2 cups worcestershire sauce
6 1-lb. pkg. brown gravy mix
3 1-lb. pkg. mushroom gravy mix
6 T. garlic powder
Tabasco to taste
Water as needed (several gallons)

This recipe fills two-22" Dutch ovens and two-17" ovens. Divide the quantities between the ovens. You need to have coals ready and begin cooking about 3 hours before serving time. Brown ground beef, and add onions and cook about 20 minutes. Then add carrots, and then potatoes, celery and cauliflower until all raw vegetables have been added. You have to be careful to bring the ovens back to a boil and cook for awhile, before adding additional vegetables. Add water as needed to give sufficient quantity, but this is a stew, not a soup. When the vegetables are about done, add the seasonings. Then add the canned and frozen vegetables (thawed). As soon as these last vegetables are hot, you are ready to serve.

FROM THE CHEF'S NOTEBOOK

Soups and stews make wonderful meals. Use the Dumpling recipe in this book to top any of them. This is an easy way to add bread to the meal, and is very delicious.

Vegetable Stew or Soup

2 28 oz. canned stewed tomatoes
1 46 oz. can V-8 juice
1 cup water for stew, 6 cups for soup
3 T. chicken or beef bouillon base
2 cups chopped onion
8 branch ends celery leaves
12 sprigs parsley
4 T. oregano
1 large bay leaf
8 cups vegetables
  zucchini
  corn on the cob
  green beans
  crookneck squash
  peas
  green peppers

Combine everything and mix well. Bring to boil, then simmer for about 1 hour. Use 12" or 14" oven. Use 16-18 coals bottom, no coals top.

Hint: There are almost limitless combinations possible. In the winter, when a lot of fresh vegetables are more scarce, use carrots, potatoes and cabbage for the vegetables and marjoram as the herb. In spring, before everything is available, use the new asparagus, mushrooms and leeks for the vegetables, or parsnips, winter squash, broccoli

"It breathes reassurance, it offers consolation; after a weary day , it promotes sociability... There is nothing like a bowl of hot soup, its wisp of aromatic steam teasing the nostrils into quivering anticipation."
-The Soup Book, Louis P. DeGouy, 1949

or cauliflower for the vegetable and basil for the herb. Pumpklin, celery and sweet onions, with cinnamon and nutmeg is a great combination. Remember all of the vegetables that are available: asparagus, broccoli, cabbage, carrots, cauliflower, celery, corn on the cob, fennel, green beans, kohlrabi, leeks, mushrooms, okra, onions, parsnips, peas, potatoes, rutabagas, sorrel, spinach, winter squash, sweet potatoes, turnips, and zucchini.

Whipped Honey Butter

2/3 cup butter
2/3 cup honey
1 egg yolk
1 1/2 t. vanilla

Soften butter. Place all ingredients in mixing bowl and beat with electric mixer until butter is light and fluffy. Serve with warm breads.

Hint: You can make different flavors of butters. Use you imagination.

FLAVORED BUTTERS

Mustard-Basil Butter made with 8 T. butter, 1/4 c. prepared mustard & 1/4 c. chopped fresh basil leaves; Dill Butter made with 8 T. butter, 3 T. chopped fresh dill, 1/2 t. lemon juice, 1/2 t. prepared mustard; Herb Butter is made with 8 T. butter & 1 T. finely chopped fresh herb of your choice.Use these on sandwiches, with fish, meat and vegetable dishes. Some fruit butters which are great on fruit breads, pancakes and waffles, muffins or biscuits are; Orange Butter made with 8 T. butter, 1/3 c. orange marmalade, 1/2 t. confectioners' sugar, grated zest of 1 orange; Strawberry Butter is 8 T. butter, 1/3 c.strawberry jam, 1/2 t. lemon juice,1/2 t. sugar.

Chapter 6

Vegetables

"NOTES"

_____

_____

_____

_____

_____

_____

_____

_____

_____

_____

_____

_____

_____

_____

_____

_____

_____

_____

CHEESES

Cheeses are a great ingredient in cooking. By choosing the kind of cheese you want, you can change the entire flavor of a dish. There are a great many varieties of cheeses available. As you try different cheeses, keep track of the flavors and how you like them. Try them in different dishes.

Cheese Stuffed Peppers

8 large green, red or yellow bell peppers
10 slices bacon, cut in 1" pieces
5 T. bacon drippings
4 cups vegetables
  whole kernel corn, cooked
  pimento
  green onion, chopped
4 cups cooked white rice
2/3 cup peanuts
2 t. thyme
2 cups plain yogurt
2 cups cheddar cheese, shredded

Cook rice in Dutch oven. (You can do this dish with one Dutch oven in steps, or two ovens, if you want to cut the cooking time down). Cut peppers in half lengthwise. Remove seeds and membrane. In oven, cook bacon until crisp. Remove and drain on paper towels. Keep bacon drippings in oven. Add vegetables. Cook until they are tender. Stir in bacon, rice, nuts and seasonings. Mix well. Fold in yogurt and cheese. Spoon rice mixture into peppers. Bake in 350 F. oven for about 50 minutes or until heated through. Use 6-8 coals bottom, 14-18 coals top.

Hint: You can substitute carrots, chopped celery, chopped onion and mushrooms, brown rice, sunflower kernels and savory with Swiss cheese and have another great dish. Or substitute chopped onion, chopped zucchini, chopped tomatoes and sliced olives, saffron-rice, pecans, and oregano with mozzarella cheese.

Honey-Ginger Baked Beans

7-8 cups navy, kidney, pinto or garbanzo beans
1 8oz. can crushed pineapple
9 slices bacon, cooked, crumbled
1/2 cup honey
1/2 cup molasses
1 1/2 cups chopped onion
2 t. dry mustard
1 t. ground ginger
2 cups liquid (from soaking beans)

Soak beans overnight in water with 1/4 t. baking soda and 1 t. salt. Drain, but reserve all liquid. Combine beans in 12" to 14" oven with pineapple in its juice, bacon, honey, molasses, onion, dry mustard and ginger. Stir in about 1 1/2 cups of soaking liquid. Mix and cover. Bake at 300 F. for about 3 hours, stirring occasionally. If additional liquid is needed, use more of the soaking liquid. Use 6-7 coals, bottom and 12-14 coals top. Serves 10-12.

OLIVES

Olives are great by themselves or in a great variety of dishes. Because there are a lot of different varieties, you can vary the flavor of the dish.

Creamed Vegetables

2 T. Roux
1/2 t. celery salt
1/4 t. white pepper
1 t. dill seed
3 cups whole milk
8 cups hot drained cooked vegetables
  peas
  new potatoes

Cook vegetables desired, drain, remove and cover to keep warm. Add roux to oven and heat, adding milk and seasonings until smooth and thick. Add vegetables and stir, coating all vegetables.

Hint: You can cream most vegetables. Some good combinations I like are carrots and onions with savory for seasoning, asparagus with tarragon for seasoning is delicious, or sliced mushrooms, leeks and yellow summer squash with dry mustard as the seasoning. There are a lot of combinations. Have fun trying them out. You can add cheeses to achieve different flavors also. Add this during the sauce preparation until cheese is combined, then add the cooked vegetables. You can make a wonderful vegetable pie by following the directions for chicken pot pie (pg. 59), but combining the

FROM THE CHEF'S NOTEBOOK

When making your white sauce, whisking the roux and milk mixture during cooking prevents the flour from lumping in the sauce. You don't want to whisk rapidly or the sauce will break down. The white sauce will thicken more as it cools. You can use the white sauces as a base for cream soups, over meat, poultry, fish or vegetables. Just use it plain, or add different flavors to complement the dish it is being used on.

vegetables you want in the cream sauce and then putting it in the pie shell.

Deep-Fried Vegetables

Batter: makes 2 cups
1 cup flour
1 cup milk
2 eggs
1/2 t. celery salt
vegetables
2-4 cups seasoned dry breadcrumbs
2 qts. vegetable oil or deep-fat frying oil
Salt to taste

Vegetables for frying:
broccoli flowerets
cauliflower flowerets
eggplant, cut in sticks
green bell pepper
mushrooms
okra
onion slices (onion rings)
zucchini, cut in sticks

In bowl, whisk together flour, milk, egg, and celery salt until smooth. Dip vegetable pieces in batter, then roll in crumbs. Heat oil in 12" oven. Should be about 375 F. Fry vegetable pieces, a few at a time, until golden brown. Turn once if necessary. Remove vegetables

FROM THE CHEF'S NOTEBOOK

To keep deep-fried pieces warm while frying remaining pieces, place in a Dutch oven with 2-3 coals on the bottom and 2-3 on the lid.

POTATOES

New, potatoes are cooked with their jackets on. More vitamins are retained that way. There are many ways to prepare potatoes. Learn to enjoy them all.

with a slotted spoon and drain on paper towels. Use 18-20 coals on bottom only.

Scalloped Potatoes Royale

6 cups sliced potatoes, with skins
1/4 cup green pepper, diced
1/4 cup green onion, diced
1/4 cup pimento
1 lb. cheddar cheese, shredded
20 oz.   cream of celery soup
10 oz   chicken broth
1/4 cup cooked corn
1 cup sour cream
1/2 cup corn flakes, crushed

Boil potatoes for 20 minutes, then drain well. Saute green peppers, and onions. Mix in sauteed green peppers, green onions with corn and pimento and cheese. Mix soup, broth, and sour cream and pour over potatoes. Bake for 1 hr and top with crushed corn flakes and shredded cheese to serve. Serves 8-12. Use 12" Dutch oven.

Spinach & Ricotta Stuffed Tomatoes

7-8 Ripe red tomatoes
1 1/2 cup finely chopped yellow onions

salt and pepper to taste
nutmeg to taste
3 eggs
1/3 cup grated Parmesan cheese
plus additional to top tomatoes
Pasta of your choice
Salt to drain tomatoes
5 T. butter
15 oz. frozen spinach, drained, dry
2 cups ricotta cheese
3/4 cup toasted pine nuts
3/4 cup chopped parsley
1 cup fresh mushrooms

Wash and dry tomatoes, cut off tops, and with spoon clean out seeds and partitions. Salt cavities and set to drain 30 minutes. Heat 1/2 of butter in Dutch oven and add onions. Cook until tender and lightly colored, about 20 minutes. Chop and add spinach to onions. Combine thoroughly, season to taste with salt, pepper and nutmeg. Cover and cook about 10 minutes. Don't' let scorch. Remove and reserve. Add other 1/2 of butter to oven and add mushrooms. Saute until done. Remove. Beat ricotta and eggs together thoroughly in bowl. Add spinach mixture, pine nuts, 1/3 cup parmesan cheese and parsley. Mix thoroughly. Season to taste with salt and pepper. Gently blot tomato cavities dry with paper towel. Spoon equal share of filling

TOMATOES

Every year, vine-ripened tomatoes are eagerly awaited. Eating them fresh off the vine with a little salt or marinated with fresh herbs - pure heaven. Preserve them as best you can for winter use.

into tomatoes and top with additional Parmesan. Arrange vegetables in shallow baking dish, or bottom of dutch oven. Bake about 20 minutes or until tops are brown and filing is bubbly hot. At the same time, in another oven, prepare pasta of your choice, as directed, using bottom heat only to boil your water. Serve your stuffed tomatoes with pasta. Use 12" Dutch oven with 6 coals bottom and 12-14 coals top. Serves 7-8.

Hint: You can also use this same recipe for stuffed peppers, only it will take a little longer to cook the peppers than the tomatoes.

Steamed Vegetables

Cut up vegetables of your choice:
Squash
mushrooms
bell peppers
onions
carrots, etc.

Place steamer in bottom of Dutch oven. Add enough water to cover bottom. Add vegetables and put on lid. Use bottom heat to boil water and steam vegetables. On 12" oven, use about 10-12 coals. Cook to desired tenderness.

LEMON BUTTER

For a delicious accompaniment to steamed vegetables, melt 8 T. of butter with the juice of 2 lemons and 2 T. freshly chopped parsley. Either use as a dip, or pour over and lightly toss the vegetables to coat with the butter.

Twice Baked Potatoes

5 medium sized potatoes
1 head broccoli
16 mushrooms, sliced
2 T. minced onions
1/2 cup butter
3/4 cup heavy cream
1 t. salt
1/2 t. pepper
colby cheese, grated
paprika

Scrub potatoes, oil skins lightly, and place on rack in 12" Dutch oven. Bake with about 15 coals on bottom and 18 on top, for about 1 hour or until done. Remove and let cool. Saute minced onions, in 2 T. butter until clear. Add mushrooms and cook until tender. Set aside to cool. Wash broccoli, chop to desired size and steam for 8-10 minutes. Remove from oven and place in cold water to stop cooking process. Set aside. Cut baked potatoes in half. Carefully remove insides and place in bowl with butter, cream, salt and pepper. Whip until fluffy. Layer whipped potatoes, mushroom and onion mixture, and broccoli in potato shells. Top with cheese and sprinkle with paprika. Return to hot oven for 10-15 minutes or until heated through. Serves 10.

BE CREATIVE

There are a variety of ingredients you can use with this dish. You can use different vegetables, sour cream instead of heavy cream, olives, mild green chili peppers, different varieties of cheeses etc. Have fun trying different combinations.

Vegetable Sundae

5-6 yellow summer squash (with 4"
base)
2 bunches broccoli
5-6 cherry tomatoes
3 T. chopped cashews
2 cups water
1 t. salt

Sauce:
Use Cheese Sauce recipe and add
3/4 cup shredded Swiss cheese, and
1/2 cup milk and 4 T. grated
parmesan where cheese is
indicated in recipe.

LEMONADE

If you want to
make real
lemonade to have
with your meal,
just mix the juice
of 12 lemons with
1/2 cup of sugar,
stirring until the
sugar dissolves.
Add the lemon
rinds, cut into
strips, and fill the
pitcher with ice.
Let the ice melt
for about 30
minutes. Serve
with a lemon slice
and a sprig of
fresh mint. This
is a great treat to
have while Dutch
oven cooking!

Trim base of squash so squash will
sit up straight in oven. Measure
up from base 2 1/2 inches and cut
to form a bowl. Hollow out seed
and pulp, leaving walls 1/2" thick.
Cut and trim broccoli leaving 1"
stems below flowery tops. Heat 2
cups water with 1 t. salt in oven.
Bring to boil. Add squash and
broccoli. Cook for 5-10 minutes
until beginning of tender stage.
Carefully remove vegetables to
drain. Discard water. Set
vegetables aside. Melt butter in
oven over low heat. Blend in flour,
salt and pepper. Cook for a few
minutes. Add milk all at once.
Cook quickly, stirring constantly,
till mixture thickens and bubbles.
Cook one additional minute and

remove sauce from heat. Add cheeses and stir until smooth. Set sauce aside while vegetables are reheated. Arrange squash cups in clean oven and fill with broccoli flowerets. Add 1/2 cup water to bottom of pot. Cover and return t heat for 5 minutes. To serve, spoon 1/4 cup of sauce over each vegetable cup. Sprinkle with 1 1/2 t. chopped cashews. Place a cherry tomato in the center.

Hints: This recipe can be adapted easily by using different types of appropriate squash bowls, vegetable fillings, and cheese sauces. Have fun.

Most dishes in this book can be prepared for large groups by using bigger ovens. The 22" oven above is sitting on a custom stand made from a barrel bottom. This puts the oven at a very workable height.

SUGAR SNAP PEAS

These are the sweetest of young peas. Wash and dry them off lightly, and discard anything that is not green. Saute them in melted butter for about 3 minutes and then serve. This is a great vegetable with any meat dish.

Chapter 7

Breads & Rolls

"NOTES"

"Bread deals with living things, with giving life, with growth, with the seed, the grain that nurtures. It is not coincidence that we day bread is the staff of life."
-Lionel Poilane

Biscuits

2 cups Dry Baking Mix (pg. 104)
1/2 cup water

Mix well until all liquid has been absorbed. Pat out or roll on a floured surface, leaving dough about 1/2 inch thick. Cut using biscuit cutter or soup can. Grease Dutch oven lightly. Place biscuits in oven. Brush tops of biscuits with melted butter if desired. Bake in a 12" oven with 7-8 coals bottom and 16-18 coals top for 10-15 minutes.

Hints: Biscuits, topped with a white sauce mix and chipped beef, makes a great meal. Try different ideas.

FROM THE CHEF'S NOTEBOOK

Fritters can be made with a variety of ingredients besides corn. I have always enjoyed them made with fruit cocktail, apple chunks, bananas, blueberries, etc.

Corn Fritters

2 cups proofed Sourdough Batter
1 1/2 cups flour
1 cup corn meal
1 cup defrosted frozen corn kernels
1 T. sugar
1/4 t. salt
1/2 t. baking soda
1 T. baking powder
1 cup milk
3 eggs, beaten
1/4 cup melted butter

Mix all ingredients together and allow to sit for about an hour before cooking.

Heat oil in 10" Dutch oven, using 12-15 coals. When a drop of water sizzles, the oil is hot enough to cook in. Drop balls of batter about the size of a walnut into the oil. Cook until they float and are golden brown. Turn them as needed. Be careful not to put too many in at one time, as this will cool the oil too fast to fry properly.

Dry Baking Mix

2 cups flour
1 T. sugar
1 T. baking powder
1/2 t salt
1/3 cup lard or shortening

Sift or mix dry ingredients. Cut in lard until mixture resembles fine meal.

Hints: This is similar to Bisquick, so you could also use this for many different applications. You can use it to make cake mixes, muffins, cookies, coffee cake, pancakes and many others. You may want to add a little sugar and eggs depending on the item you choose.

BREAD FLOUR

Flours are now being marketed by major millers that are especially formulated to duplicate professional bakers' flour. It is not always available in all markets, but it has superior flavor and texture and is worth finding. If it is not stocked in your market, ask them to stock it.

Dumplings

2 1/2 cups flour
3 t. baking powder
1 t. salt
3 T. Crisco
2 T. chopped parsley
1 cup milk
2 eggs

Mix dry ingredients and cut in Crisco, using a pastry blender, until mixture is coarse and grainy. Add parsley, and with a wooden fork, stir in the milk only until mixed. Drop by spoonfuls on top of the simmering prepared item for dumplings. Simmer 5 minutes with the lid off and then cover and simmer 15-20 minutes. Serve immediately.

Hint: Dumplings are great on all kinds of dishes. Use them on soups, stews, fruit, for a dessert, and of course, they make great chicken and dumplings.

Fantastic Hard Rolls

3 1/2 cups flour
2 pkgs active dry yeast
1 t. salt
1 t. sugar
1 1/2 cups warm water
1 egg white

poppy seeds if desired

Mix flour, yeast and salt together in bowl. Add warm water and mix well to a good dough consistency. Let rise till double. Divide into 8-12 rolls and shape. Let rise again. Bake for 30 minutes. Spray with water 3 times in the first 10 minutes during baking. After 20 minutes, brush with egg white and sprinkle on poppy seeds. Finish cooking until golden brown. Cook with 8 coals on bottom and 15-18 top. Serves 6-8. Use 12" Dutch oven.

Potato Rolls

1 1/2 cups warm water
3/4 cup sugar
1 pkg. active dry yeast
2/3 cup instant potatoes
2/3 cup hot water
1 1/2 t. salt
2/3 cup soft shortening
3 eggs
7 cups flour (as needed)

Mix 1st amount of warm water and sugar in large bowl. Sprinkle yeast into mixture and set aside to work. Mix instant potatoes and hot water. Set aside to cool. When yeast is dissolved, add salt, shortening, eggs and cooled

COOKOUT CHECKLIST

_Tablecloth
_Flatware, plates
_Glasses, cups
_Thermos and ice
_Sharp knife
_Cutting board
_Serving platter
_Napkins
_Paper towels
_Matches
_Charcoal
_Dutch ovens
_Utensils/cooking
_Coal bucket
_Shovel
_Whisk broom
_Garbage bags
_Spatula
_Candles or
_Flashlight
_First-aid kit
_Etc.

SOURDOUGH

This is probably the oldest form of "raised" bread that we know of. It is a wild yeast form. There is some evidence that Columbus brought a sourdough starter with him on the ships that set out for the New World. It has been used in the United States since the beginning. Pioneers used it and during the Alaskan gold rush, it was constantly used. Many people have starters that are from this time period, and are still being used.

potatoes. Mix well. Add two cups flour and beat until smooth. Cover with towel and let rest 10 minutes. Mix in remaining flour until dough is easy to handle. Turn onto a lightly floured surface and knead until smooth and elastic. Place in a greased bowl and turn dough so greased side is up. Cover with damp cloth and let rise until double, about 1 1/2 hours. Shape into rolls and place in oven. Let rise until double. Makes about 24 rolls. Bake 15-20 minutes with 7-8 coals bottom and 15-18 on top. Use 12" or 14" Dutch oven.

Hint: When needing to raise rolls, you can place 2-3 coals on your lid, and this will heat it enough to speed up the rise.

Sourdough French Bread

Mix and dissolve in large bowl:
2 T. sugar
1 pkg. active dry yeast
1 1/2 cup hot water
Add:
1 cup sourdough start
1/2 t. salt
2 cups flour

Mix well for two minutes with electric beater, then let sit and rest for 10 minutes.

Add:
1/2 t. soda
2 1/2 to 3 more cups of flour (as needed)

Mix well and continue kneading 5 to 10 minutes or until satiny in appearance. Place in greased bowl and let rise in warm spot until doubled in volume. Knead down and let rise again. Form into desired shape and let rise until doubled. Bake for 35-45 minutes at 400 F. On a 12" or 14" Dutch oven, use 6-8 coals bottom, 16-18 coals top.

Sourdough Batter w/Milk

to your start add:
1 cup <u>whole</u> milk
1 cup flour
1/4 to 1/3 cup sugar

Mix and let stand for at least 3 hours (or better, over night). Before using, remove one cup as "start" and proceed with recipe as directed. For best results, start should be divided only once a week and no more. Save start in mason jar or crock and store in refrigerator. If properly cared for, start will keep for 6-9 months with little or no attention.

FROM THE CHEF'S NOTEBOOK

Once you have your sourdough start going, here is one recipe for making the batter that you bake with, reserving part as your start. This is one my friend Joan uses. She says you have to use whole milk, or it won't work.

Sourdough Starter

If you can get a start from
someone, that is great. If you want
to start from scratch here is how to
do it.

1 cup water
1 T. sugar
1 cup flour
4 T. buttermilk

Mix water and sugar together.
Add flour and buttermilk. Place in
glass or stainless-steel bowl. Do
not use aluminum. Cover with a
towel and allow to stand in warm
spot for a few days, or until it has
begun to ferment (has a sour
smell)

Sourdough Batter w/Water

You need to think ahead, because
the batter needs to be made about
12 hours before you begin the
bread-making process. Allow
starter to come to room
temperature.

1 1/2 cups starter
1 1/2 cups flour
1 cup tepid water

Mix ingredients a 2-quart bowl.
Cover, and allow to sit out
overnight and the "batter" will be

ready to use the next day. Use the amount of batter called for in the recipe and return the rest to the starter bowl in the refrigerator. Always remember to add back to your starter, what you take out to keep it in good supply. Add back the same amount of flour and water, mix it up and put it in the starter bowl.

Tasty Dinner Rolls

2 cups hot water, cool to lukewarm
1/2 cup melted margarine
1/2 cup sugar
2 t. salt
2 eggs
2 T. dry active yeast
1/4 cup lukewarm water
5 1/2 cups flour.

Mix together well. Let rise 1 hour. Knead, Shape Let rise, Bake. Use 14" dutch oven. Use 6-8 coals bottom, 15-18 coals top. Bake for about 15-20 minutes or until golden brown. Use 12" or 14" Dutch oven. Serves 12-14.

Whole Wheat Bread

1 pkg active dry yeast
1/3 cup lukewarm water
3 t. shortening

BREAD BOX

You can make a giant loaf of bread in your Dutch oven, like Sheepherder bread. Hollow it out and fill it with a stew, soup or sandwiches. Cut off the top of the loaf with a serrated knife and reserve the top. Carefully pull out the soft interior of the loaf, leaving the crust intact. The soft interior would work wonderfully for the bread in the Mock Cheese & Sausage Souffle (pg. 47). Or you can roll pieces flat with a rolling pin and then cut them into shapes with cookie cutters. Use these shapes to make sandwiches. They are a lot of fun.

4 t. honey
4 t. molasses
3 t. salt
3 Cups milk, scalded
6 cups wholewheat flour

Soften yeast in water. Melt shortening and combine with honey, molasses, salt and scalded milk. Cook to lukewarm and combine with yeast mixture. Add flour enough to make a soft dough and knead thoroughly, using extra flour as needed. Shape in rolls and place in oven. Let rise not quite double. Bake at 350 F. with 6-8 coals bottom and 15-18 coals top for 12" oven. Bake about 30-35 minutes or until done.

Wild Onion Bread

1 1/2 oz. pkg. onion soup mix
3/4 cup hot water
1 pkg. active dry yeast
2 T. sugar
2 T. warm water
1 egg
2 recipes Dry Baking Mix (pp 104)
1 cup sour dough

"Looks can be deceiving - it's eating that's believing."
-James Thurber

Add soup mix to 3/4 cup hot water; let stand until lukewarm. In separate container, soften yeast and sugar with 2 T. warm water. Beat soup mixture and yeast mixture together with egg, 1 cup Dry Baking Mix and sourdough starter. Let rest for 10 minutes. Stir in remaining Dry Baking Mix to make dough stiff. Place on a floured surface; knead until smooth and elastic. Place in greased bowl, turn to grease top. Cover and let rise for 2 hours. Shape into a round loaf. Place in 12" Dutch oven. Let rise about 45 minutes. Bake at 375 F. for about 35 minutes. 6-8 coals bottom, 15-18 coals top. Makes 1 loaf.

PECANS

Pecans were introduced to early colonists by the Indians. The nut meat is very flavorful, making it versatile in cooking and baking because it blends so well with other foods. If you lightly toast pecans before using, it will intensify their flavor. They are great in sweet rolls, sticky buns, muffins, fruit salads, stuffings, etc.

Find dishes you like and try preparing them the Dutch oven way. The filling in the Pita sandwiches above was prepared in the Dutch oven.

Chapter 8

Desserts

"NOTES"

Baked Apples

1 apple per person (be sure to use a baking apple)
raisins
brown sugar
butter
cinnamon

Core apples, but leave bottom intact. Mix raisins and brown sugar together, so that raisins are well coated. Spoon mixture into apples. Sprinkle a little cinnamon on the top. Place a dab of butter on the top. Place apples in oven, with a little water. Bake about 20-30 minutes, using medium heat.

Blueberry Cake

1/3 cup butter
1 cup sugar
1/8 t. cinnamon
1/2 cup sour milk or buttermilk
1 egg
2 cups flour
1 t. baking soda
2 cups blueberries

BLUEBERRIES

Robert Frost called these dewy bunches of blue "a vision of thieves," though they needn't be stolen to be enjoyed. We are thankful that cultivators have made blueberries readily available.

Preheat 12" Dutch oven with rack. Cream butter until light, add sugar and continue creaming until fluffy. Beat in egg. Sift together flour, soda, and cinnamon. Add alternately with the buttermilk to the creamed mixture, beginning and ending with the dry ingredients. The batter will be stiff, but it must be to support the weight of the blueberries to be added. Pick over the berries, discarding stems and any green or withered ones, but do not defrost if using frozen berries. Stir into batter and spread in well-greased 9x9x2" square or a deep 9" round pan. Place cake in preheated oven on the rack, and bake until toothpick comes out of the cake clean. Cook about 50-60 minutes at 350 F. 6-8 coals bottom, 14-16 coals top. If you want, you could cook it in 10" oven, well greased and floured, with the same procedure, eliminating the pan and rack. Serves 6-8.

Cobbler Delight

1 #2 1/2 can sliced peaches
1 #2 1/2 can fruit cocktail
1 smaller can crushed pineapple
1/2 cup instant tapioca
1/4 lb. butter
1 cup brown sugar
1 dry cake mix

In 12" oven, mix fruit and tapioca. (If you prefer, line your oven with foil first, for easy clean-up). Sprinkle cake mix evenly over top

BERRIES

One season that comes and goes too fast, is the berry season. As soon as you notice they are in the markets, they vanish. Berries are wonderful to eat as they are, or added to make a different dish, or great with whipped cream. Eat one alone, or combined with others in hundreds of ways.

of fruit. Sprinkle brown sugar over cake. Dab butter all over top of brown sugar. Place lid on oven. Bake for about 45 minutes to an hour. Use 6-8 coals on the bottom and 14-16 on the top. It is done, when top is brown and cake has absorbed juices and is no longer dry.

Hints: Cobbler can be prepared a lot of different ways. Use pie fillings instead of regular fruit and omit the tapioca. Use a mixed cake batter instead of the dry cake and omit the brown sugar and butter topping. You test to see if it is done with a toothpick, just like a regular cake. There are a lot of different combinations. Try different ones and find the ones you prefer. All you have to do is keep the proportions about the same as the above recipe for a 12" oven.

Fruit Pizza

Crust:
2 cups all-purpose flour
1 t. salt
1/4 cup vegetable shortening
1 t. vinegar
1 egg
1 to 2 T. Water

Sift flour and salt together into bowl. Add shortening and blend with with pastry blender until it resembles meal. Add vinegar and egg and mix. Add water, a tablespoon at a time, until ingredients hold together. Roll out the pastry on a floured surface to fit bottom of dutch oven. Place on pizza pan to fit in oven or place directly on bottom of oven. Cook at 400 F. for 15-20 minutes or until lightly browned. 10-12 coals bottom, 15-18 coals top. Remove and let cool. Use 14" or 16" Dutch oven. This will allow a good sized pizza pan to fit.

Topping:
Cool whip or favorite whipped topping
strawberries
grapes
Bananas
mandarin oranges
fruits that are in season

When crust is cool, spread whipped topping on as thick as you would like. Then arrange cut up fruit in design on top of whipped topping. Be creative.

Hints: Sugar cookie dough that you can buy already prepared, is also an excellent crust for this fun

"Long live the sun which gives us such beautiful color."
-Paul Cezanne

dessert. Spread cookie dough in bottom of oven and proceed the same way.

Pineapple Up-side-down Cake

1/2 cube butter
2/3 cup brown sugar
12-16 pineapple slices
12-16 maraschino cherry halves
1 cake mix, prepared, following recipe

In 12" oven (line with foil if preferred) heat butter and brown sugar in bottom until melted and well mixed. Place pineapple rings on top of butter-sugar mixture and put cherries in the middle of the pineapple rings. Pour the prepared cake batter over the top. Cook with 7-8 coals on the bottom and 16-18 on top. Cook for 45 minutes or until cake tests done. Turn up-side-down to serve.

Raspberry Supreme Crepes

6 eggs
1/4 t. salt
2 T. water
1/4 cup all-purpose flour

FROM THE CHEF'S NOTEBOOK

Raspberries are the most elegant berry of all. They have been cherished for centuries and they never seem to be abundant or affordable enough to be taken for granted. Enjoy them with a bit of cream or plain. What a pleasure!

3 T. powdered sugar

Combine eggs, salt and water in bowl and beat thoroughly. Sift flour and sugar together, then beat into the egg mixture gradually until smooth. To cook, place Dutch oven lid up-side-down on bricks or other support. Place coals under lid to heat. Coat lid with good layer of oil. Spoon crepe batter onto middle of lid and spread out to make a thin layer so you have a crepe about 6" across. Have thin spatula to turn crepe when done. Lift off and place on dish. Continue this process until all batter is cooked. Makes about ten 6-inch crepes.

Filling:
1 carton cool whip
1 carton fresh or frozen raspberries, or can of raspberry pie filling.

Mix together. Either spoon or use pastry bag to fill crepes. You can arrange them together on a plate and sprinkle with powdered sugar.

Hints: If you would like to use the crepes as a main dish with creamed chicken, tuna, cream cheese and shrimps or vegetables as the filling, omit the sugar in the batter and then proceed the same.

FRUIT DESSERTS

Some great fall fruits to enjoy as desserts; Seedless grapes topped with sour cream and brown sugar, lightly broiled, pear halves baked with brown sugar and chopped hazelnuts, apples baked with maple syrup, applesauce and homemade cookies, poached pears and gingerbread.

DELICIOUS FRUIT

Cakes, pies, candies, and cookies are wonderful desserts, but sometimes something a little lighter is appropriate. Try balls of honeydew, cucumbers, cantaloupe and sprinkled with fresh lemon juice and chopped mint leaves. Or try bananas, fresh pineapple chunks and cherries topped with a little orange juice.

Sour-Cream Apple Pie

Crust:
2 1/2 cups unbleached all-purpose flour
3/4 t. salt
6 T. Sweet butter, chilled
4-6 T. apple juice, chilled
5 T. granulated sugar
3/4 t. cinnamon
6 T. shortening, chilled

Sift flour, sugar, salt & cinnamon into bowl. Cut in butter & shortening with fork or pastry blender. Moisten with just enough juice to permit dough to be formed into ball. Cut off 1/3 and reserve in cool place. Roll out 2/3 dough between wax paper. Line bottom of 12-inch Dutch oven and up sides. When filling is ready, add, and then roll out top crust, cut in lattice strips and lace over top, joining lattice strips to side crusts.

Filling:
5-7 small tart apples
1/3 cup granulated sugar
1/4 t. salt
3 T. all-purpose flour
2/3 cup dairy sour cream
1 egg
1 t. vanilla extract

Peel, core and thinly slice apples; drop slices into mixing bowl.

Whisk together sour cream, sugar, egg, salt, vanilla & pour in small bowl. Pour mixture over apples & toss until well coated. Spoon apples into pastry lined oven.

Topping:
3 T. brown sugar
1 t. cinnamon
3 T. granulated sugar
1 cup chopped walnuts

Mix sugars, cinnamon & walnuts together & sprinkle evenly over apple filling. Finish top, then bake. 8-10 coals bottom, 16-20 coals top, until crust is golden brown, and filling bubbling. Serves 8-10.

Sweet Dreams Carrot Cake

4 cups flour
1 cup packed brown sugar
1 cup granulated sugar
1 t. baking powder
1 t. baking soda
1 t. salt
2 t. ground cinnamon
3 cups shredded carrots
6 eggs
1 1/2 cup vegetable oil
1 t. vanilla extract
1 cup crushed pineapple with juice
1 cup chopped walnuts

CHOCOLATE TYPES

Unsweetened dark chocolate, or baking chocolate, is most often used for cooking. Powdered cocoa, and semisweet and dark sweet chocolate also have many uses. White chocolate is wonderful for dipping and fondues. If is not really chocolate by cocoa butter, sugar and milk with additional flavorings. There are also many artificial chocolates. If you want the real thing, be sure to read labels.

1 cup coconut
1 cup raisins

Grease and flour Dutch oven. Mix all dry ingredients together well. Add carrots, eggs, oil and vanilla, stir until well combined. Stir in nuts, pineapple, raisins and coconut. Pour into 12" Dutch oven. Bake at 350 F. for 1 hour or until done. Let cool, then frost. Use 6-8 coals bottom, 12-14 coals top, moving the coals on the lid to the center to finish cooking the middle of the cake. Invert oven to remove cake.

Frosting:
1 1/2 pkg. (12oz.) cream cheese, softened
1/4 cup margarine
2 1/2 cups powdered sugar
2 T. chopped maraschino cherries
Coconut, shredded
Hot water, if needed

Cream together cream cheese, margarine, and sugar. Add cherries. Add a little hot water, 1 teaspoon at a time, until you reach spreading consistency. Mix well. Spread on cake when it is cooled. If you like, pat coconut onto the frosting and garnish with maraschino cherries.

FROM THE CHEF'S NOTEBOOK

Just like the happy endings in stories, we like similar endings to our meals. Be sure the desserets you are serving add a happy ending that is enjoyable and completes the meal to everyones satisfaction.

Whole Pumpkin Pie

1 pumpkin, 5-7 lbs.
8 whole eggs
2 cups whipping cream
2/3 cup brown sugar
1 T. molasses
1/2 t. grated nutmeg
1 t. cinnamon
1/4 t. ginger
2 T. butter

Cut lid off pumpkin, like for jack-o-lantern. Remove seeds and strings. Mix all the the other ingredients except the butter. This is a custard filling. Pour into the pumpkin and top with the butter. Place the pumpkin lid back on and place the entire pumpkin in a 15" deep or 17" deep Dutch oven. Use about 15 coals on the bottom and 25 on top for the 15" and about 17 on the bottom and 30 on the top for the 17". Bake for about 1 1/2 hours or until the mixture has set like a custard. Serve, scraping some of the pumpkin from the sides along with the custard for each serving. This is an old early American recipe used in the colonial days. Even though it is not like your traditional pie, it is excellent.

USE PUMPKINS

We all think of pumpkin at Thanksgiving time, and then many of us forget about them. They are a great vegetable, and can be used throughout most of the winter. You can use them is pies, breads, cookies, soups, cheesecakes, waffles, pancakes and in cakes. Think of other ways to use them. They also make great soup tureens, for other types of soups, utilizing it as a centerpiece also.

Chapter 9

Cooking For Groups

"NOTES"

FIRST IMPRESSIONS

When cooking for groups, first impressions often help determine the tastiness of the items the guests will be eating. It is important that a good impression is given, so the meal will taste its best.

Once word gets out that you cook in a Dutch oven, you will start to get requests to cook for your friends, work parties, church parties and others. Don't be afraid to say yes. Then enjoy the fun you will have working on the food knowing that the group will get to eat one of their finest meals ever.

I am not going to list a lot of recipes here. When I go out to cook for a group, I use recipes that are already in this book; *Stew For The Masses* (pg. 85), *Primed with Bacon* (pg. 67) or many others.

You can use any recipe in this book when cooking for groups. Just multiply the ingredients for the number you will be serving. Many times I will be using as many as 12-14 ovens for cobbler. You may be able to use a larger size Dutch oven to get more servings out of one oven. This is just a matter of simple math.

If you are serving a small group, you may want to choose a more spectacular dish like *Crown Roast of Pork* (pg.62) or *Cornish Game Hens* (pg.61), than if you are serving an entire church group of 300. Then you may want to do a stew.

As you start to cook for groups, let me give you one word of advice. Be sure you have enough help to do the job. If you don't, you can drive yourself crazy in one meal.

Be aware that in most cities, there are companies that serve the restaurant industry and sell prepared vegetables. These are already washed, pealed where necessary, and cut up. You pay a little extra for this service, but it is well worth it for the time saved.

Institutional food suppliers (ones who supply the food industry with their canned goods and frozen products) are great sources for ingredients when cooking for large groups. Find one in your area, and try them out. Ask questions about what they carry so you will know how to plan your meal.

Plan out your meal on paper right down to the minute you plan to do each step, and your meal will go just fine. Good Luck and have fun.

"Small cheer and great welcome makes a merry feast."
-William Shakespeare

FROM THE CHEF'S NOTEBOOK

Whenever possible, serve a wide variety of foods. People like to eat lightly, and taste a lot of different flavors.

When cooking for groups, survey the location for the most suitable cooking site.

Chapter 10

Old Deseret Cookoff

NOTE: For the last three years, on or around the 24th of July, there has been an Old Deseret Cookoff at Pioneer Trails State Park. Because we have competed and been involved in this project, we have been able to include for you in this book, the recipes that were prepared for this competition in 1987 and 1988. The hints in the columns have been added by the author, and are not part of the recipes. We hope you enjoy these dishes as much as we have. Thanks to all of the contestants who make these competitions so educational and fun. The names of the contestants who prepared the dishes are included for your information. We have not named the winners, because all of the recipes are great, and depending on conditions, all of us have had recipes fail to turn out the way we want.

"NOTES"

GARLIC

Garlic is the strongest-flavored member of the onion group. They should be firm and crisp. The fresher the garlic, the milder the taste. Raw garlic, minced or forced through a press, retains its pungent flavor and odor. Cooked garlic becomes more subtle the longer it is exposed to heat.

Main Dishes

Barbecued Sweet and Sour Spareribs

2-3 lbs. spareribs
Salt and pepper
1/4 cup chopped celery
1/4 cup chopped green pepper
1/4 cup chopped onion
2 t. cornstarch
2 cup crushed pineapple
2 T. butter
2 t. soy sauce
1/4 t. powdered chopped garlic or clove
1/4 t. ground ginger
1 cup water
1/4 cup vinegar

Salt and pepper spareribs and cook in oven for 1 hour. Drain off fat. Cook onion, celery, and green pepper in butter until tender. Sprinkle cornstarch over vegetables. Add remaining ingredients. Cook until mixture is clear and thickened. Spoon over spareribs. Return to oven. Cover and cook at about 350 F. for 1 hour or until done. If crisp ribs are desired, do not cover, but baste them often.

Prepared by Steven Heward
1987 Cookoff

Brigham Stew

3 rabbits, cut in serving size
5 carrots, diced oblique
2 large onions, diced
1 large leek, shaved
1/2 bunch celery, sliced
1 cube butter
1 1/2 cups mushrooms, sliced
4 cups tomatoes, diced (8 medium)
2 T. Rosemary
4 Bay leaves
1 T. rubbed sage
Salt and pepper to taste

Saute vegetables in the butter until onions are translucent, but still firm. Sear meat at high temperature to hold in moisture. Add to vegetables. Add mushrooms, tomatoes, and seasonings. Simmer until meat is tender and falling off the bone. Add water if needed. (Cook about 2 hours)

Prepared by Jager Family
1988 Cookoff

Chicken Fantasia

Mix in oven:
3/4 cup maraschino cherry juice
1/2 t. salt
3/4 cup brown sugar
1/4 cup lemon juice

FROM THE CHEF'S NOTEBOOK

When game was plentiful, all families hunted as a matter of course. Many people still prize game. We now have to raise our own or go the butcher to supply the materials.

1 T. Soy sauce
1/4 t. paprika
1/2 t. ginger
juice from 1 small can mandarin oranges
1 pkg. sweet and sour mix

bring to boil:
2 T. cornstarch mixed with 1/4 cup pineapple juice, add for thickening
then, set in bowl to cool, cover

Brown 10-12 small chicken breasts in 1/2 inch oil, drain off excess oil, add 1/2 cup water.

FROM THE CHEF'S NOTEBOOK

Chicken today is easy on the pocketbook and on the calorie-counter. It is a very popular item. We don't want it to become dull. Try lots of different ways to prepare chicken. It is compatible with so many different seasonings and cooking methods, that it will only be dull, if you want it to be.

Add to thickened mixture the following:
1 cup pineapple chunks
1/2 cup diced green peppers
1/2 cup maraschino cherries
1 cup sliced carrots
1 cup sliced celery
1/2 cup chopped red sweet onion
1 8-ounce sliced water chestnuts
1 small can mandarin oranges (juice drained off)

pour over chicken. Steam over low heat for 1 hour. Stir often.

Prepared by Ryan Larsen & Bryan Harding
1988 Cookoff

Chicken with Rice

6 boneless chicken breasts
12 slices wafer thin ham
6 slices bacon
2 cups rice
2 cups milk
2 cans cream of mushroom soup
10 carrots peeled and sliced
1 pint fresh mushrooms

Wrap chicken in ham and wrap bacon around bundle. Place 2 cups milk in bottom of Dutch oven and pour rice over milk. Arrange chicken in center on top of rice, carrots, around edge, and mushrooms surrounding carrots and chicken. Spread mushroom soup over top of entire arrangement. Cover and cook on coals 50-60 minutes. Put 6-8 coals on bottom and 14-16 on top.

Prepared by Bob Kinney
1987 Cookoff

Deep Fried Pizza

Pizza Dough:
1 pkg. active dry yeast
1 cup warm water (105-115)
1 t. salt
1 t. vegetable oil
2 1/2 cups flour

WILD RICE

Wild rice is a distinguished native food of North America. It has slender ash-brown to blackish grains and a nutty taste.

Dissolve yeast in warm water. Stir in remaining ingredients; beat vigorously 20 strokes. Let rest about 5 minutes.

Pizza Sauce:
2 8oz. cans tomato sauce
1 or 2 cloves of fresh garlic
2 T. chopped onion
1/2 t. italian seasoning
1 T. oil

Heat oil; add garlic and brown. Add onions and saute. Add tomato sauce and italian seasoning. Cook to desired consistency.

Pizza:
Pepperoni
Olives
Mushrooms
Pineapple
Mozzarella cheese

Take a small ball of pizza dough, roll it out into a 5 inch circle. Place cheese, and whatever topping you like on half the circle. Be careful not to put too much on, or it will burst while cooking. Fold empty half over topping and seal tightly by pinching edges together. Place into preheated oil (350 F.) let cook until golden brown. Remove carefully to avoid splatters, and place on paper towels to drain,

"There is no love sincerer than the love of Food."
-George Bernard Shaw

then place on plate, and top with pizza sauce, and if desired more grated cheese.

Prepared by Anderton Family
1988 Cookoff

Fish Chowder

3/4 cup diced potatoes
1/2 cup diced celery
2 T. diced onion
3/4 cup water
2 T. butter
1/2 t. salt
2 T. flour
2 cups milk
1/2 lb. (about 2 cups) cooked fish,
broken into pieces
1/2 cup tomato juice
2 T. Worcestershire Sauce

Simmer vegetables in water until tender. Melt butter over low heat, add salt and flour, and stir well. Remove from heat and gradually add milk. Cook until thick and smooth, stirring all the time. combine with vegetables,fish and any liquid used in cooking fish (or in canned fish). Add tomato juice and Worcestershire sauce. Heat well and serve. Makes 1 quart.

Prepared by a Varsity Scout Team
1988 Cookoff

POPULAR SEAFOOD VARIETIES

Freshwater:
Bass
Rainbow Trout
Perch
Whitefish

Shellfish:
Scallops
Lobster
Shrimp
Prawns
Oysters
Clams
Crabs
Crayfish

Saltwater:
Bass
Snapper
Salmon
Cod
Flounder
Swordfish

Game Hens with Herb Stuffing

1 small onion, diced
1 stalk celery, sliced
1/2 t. sage
1/2 t. parsley
1/2 t. thyme
1 clove garlic, minced
salt and pepper taste
1 cup chicken stock
4-6 slices of bread, cubed
2 cornish game hens

Saute onion and celery until transparent, add seasonings, and chicken stock. Add mixture to cubed bread, blend gently. Stuff hens. Place a small amount of water in bottom of oven to help steam hens. Baste with drippings. Cook in Dutch oven for 1- 1 1/2 hours.

Prepared by Michael Treshow VII
1987 Cookoff

Hints: Use 12-16 coals bottom, for first 15-20 minutes, then add 10-14 top and continue cooking for 40-45 minutes until leg joints move freely.

SAGE

There are over 100 different varieties of sage. They grow well outdoors or on a sunny window sill. Some are decorative and great for garnishes. It is wonderful with poultry, veal and pork. Sage is a symbol of wisdom and immortality.

Hearty Beef Pie

Crust:
2 1/4 cups flour
3/4 cup yellow cornmeal
1/2 t. salt
3/4 cup cold butter or margarine, cut into small pieces
2 large eggs
3 to 4 T. cold water

Mix flour, cornmeal and salt together. Cut in butter with pastry blender until mixture resembles course crumbs. Beat eggs with 3 tablespoons water. Stir into flour mixture until dough holds together. If still dry add a little more water. Shape about 2/3 mixture into flattened ball, wrap and refrigerate 30 minutes. Do the same with other 1/3 of dough. When dough is ready, pat 2/3 mixture ball into Dutch oven. Fill with filling. Add top crust, making several vent holes. Pinch sides together and brush with egg.

Filling:
1 1/2 lbs stew meat
1/2 lb bacon
1 onion, diced
1/2 lb carrots, sliced
1 lb peas
5 medium potatoes
3 stalks celery
2 cubes beef bouillion

CORN

Corn, a gift from the Native Americans, has saved many people from starvation during early Colonial times. Cornmeal has a great variety of uses, basic to our history. Johnny cake, cornmeal mush, fritters, corn bread, etc. These can all be prepared in the Dutch oven. Find your family favorites and try them.

1 cup water
1/3 cup soy sauce
2 T. worcestershire sauce
2 to 3 drops tabasco sauce
Cornstarch to thicken

Fry bacon, add meat and onions and brown well. Add remaining ingredients except starch. Simmer until vegetables are tender. Thicken with corn starch. Remove from oven and prepare oven for dough.
Bake pie until crust is golden brown. 6 to 10 coals bottom and 16 to 20 coals top. 35 to 40 minutes.

Prepared by Cowley Family
1988 Cookoff

FROM THE CHEF'S NOTEBOOK

Sausage makes a wonderful stuffing for mushrooms. Just add a little garlic, minced onions, parsley & chopped black olives as you cook it. Spoon into the mushrooms and bake for about 5 minutes.

Mexi Sausage Pie

1 lb. pork sausage
1 pkg. onion soup mix
3 cups water
2 cans tomato paste
1 pkg. frozen corn
2 T. chili powder
1/4 t. red pepper
1/4 t. powdered garlic
1 1/2 cups cornmeal
1 egg
3/4 cup milk

Brown sausage: drain off fat. Add soup mix, water, tomato paste, corn, and seasonings. Simmer for 5 minutes. Mix cornmeal, egg, and milk; spoon over top. Bake at 425 F. for 20 minutes.

Prepared by Paul Engel
1988 Cookoff

Prairie Chicken

1 "Prairie" chicken
1/4 cup melted butter
3 tomatoes, cut in wedges
2 green peppers, cut in rings
2 medium onions, sliced
1 clove garlic, chopped
1/4 lb. cooked smoked ham, cut up
8 black olives, cut in half
1 t. salt
1/4 t. pepper

Fasten neck skin of chicken to back with skewer. Fold wings across back with tips touching. Tie or skewer drumsticks to tail. Brush with butter. Place chicken breast side up in Dutch oven. Cook covered at 375 F. brushing with butter every 30 minutes, until thickest pieces of chicken are done, about 1 1/2 hours. Add tomatoes, green peppers, onions, garlic, ham, and olives. Sprinkle chicken and vegetables with salt and pepper. Cover and cook until green pepper

TOMATOES

If you buy fresh tomatoes in the winter, look at them carefully. Don't pick those that are too pink. When you get them home, let them set out to finish ripening.

is tender, about 20 minutes. Place chicken on serving platter: arrange vegetables and ham around chicken.

Prepared by Kinney Family
1988 Cookoff

Prairie Roll-ups with Sweet and Sour Cabbage

2 1/2 lbs Top Sirloin
8 strips bacon, chopped
1 large onion, chopped
Salt & pepper

Cut meat into 8 strips about 4 inches wide and 1/8 to 1/4 inch thick. Pound meat with cleaver or rolling pin to flatten slightly. Generously salt and pepper one side of the meat. Combine bacon and onion. Place a generous spoonful at one end of each piece of meat. Roll up jelly-roll fashion and fasten roll with skewers or toothpicks. Brown roll-ups in hot shortening in Dutch oven. When browned, add 1/2 cup water. Cover and simmer for an hour or until done into the center. Remove roll-ups and make gravy from pan drippings.

Sweet & Sour Cabbage
6 T. vinegar

FROM THE CHEF'S NOTEBOOK

When you plan your parties, or meals, they should follow a natural progression. Try to plan your courses so they proceed from one to the next in an easy flow.

3 T. brown sugar
1 1/2 tsp. salt
6 whole cloves
2 bay leaves
6 cups shredded red cabbage
1 large apple grated

Combine all ingredients and marinate 1 hour. Melt 3 T. butter in Dutch oven, and add mixture. Cover and simmer 20-30 minutes. Serve with roll-ups.

Prepared by Cook family and Woods family
1988 Cookoff

Quick Beans

2 2 1/2 size can pork and beans
1 lb. hamburger
1 medium onion
1 2 1/2 size canned tomatoes
1 green pepper
2 T. brown sugar
1 t. chili powder
savory salt to taste
salt and pepper to taste

Brown hamburger in 12" or 14" Dutch oven. Add onions and green peppers, salt, tomatoes & beans. Cover. Bring to a boil. Serve. Serves 8-10.

Prepared by Bill Davies
1987 Cookoff

THE MAYONNAISE DIFFERENCE

A fun item to try to add variety to your cooking, is to use different flavored mayonnaises. You can make your own homemade mayonnaise or use that which you get from the store. Either way, it is a lot of fun. Some of these sauces are great on meats, and a lot are great on sandwiches and in salads. You can start with 1 cup of mayonnaise and add fresh herbs, depending on what you want it to go with; basil, thyme, mint, dill, etc. Also use lemon and lime juice, tabasco sauce, salt and pepper, diced onion etc. You can add fruit juices, and this makes a great sauce served over fresh fruit salads.

Rouladen

2 large round steaks
salt, pepper, and garlic powder to
taste
mustard
small whole dill pickles
diced uncooked bacon
chopped onion
flour
butter
1/2 cup dill pickle juice
1 1/2 cup water

Trim fat from round steak and pound out thinly; cut into serving pieces approximately 2 1/2 inches by 6 inches. Season each piece with salt, pepper and garlic powder. Spread thinly with mustard. Place 1 whole pickle, 1 tablespoon bacon and 1 tablespoon chopped onion in center of each piece; roll. Tie with cotton string. Roll in flour; brown in butter. Add pickle juice and water; simmer slowly with coals on bottom only for 2 to 4 hours or until tender, turning meat occasionally. Remove string from rouladen before serving.

Hint: Serving suggestion: Arrange rouladen spoke-fashion on bed of cooked rice. Garnish with parsley, cherry tomatoes, and dill pickle chips.

TASTY PUREES

Purees often taste better than the original fruit or vegetable. They are prepared so there are no strings, seeds, or pits. Only "pure" food is left. Puree vegetables with combinations of herbs, spices, fruits, nuts and peppers. Fruits can be pureed to make a wonderful low-fat desserts.

Prepared by Jackson Family
1988 Cookoff

Sweet and Sour Ham Rolls

6 slices ham
2-3 small zucchini, julienne
2-3 small carrots, julienne
1 pkg. stuffing mix
1 pkg Sweet & Sour mix
2 T. butter
1 can fruit cocktail
toothpicks

Cut vegetables in Julienne strips, saute in butter till tender. Wrap in ham slices and fasten with toothpicks. Prepare foil bowls, and place in dutch oven. Prepare stuffing and S & S mix in foil bowls. Close foil to keep stuffing and sauce warm. Coat bottom of Dutch oven with oil. Place ham roll-ups in oven; turn until warmed through. Turn Dutch oven lid upside down and place stuffing on lid. Place ham rolls on stuffing. Pour sweet and sour sauce over ham rolls. Serve.

Prepared by Varsity Scouts
1987 Cookoff

FROM THE CHEF'S NOTEBOOK

One thing to be careful about, is not to entertain more people than you really feel comfortable with. Know your limitations and work with them. If you want to entertain large numbers, practice and work out the details ahead of time.

Stuffed Pork Chops

6 pocket pork chops - 1 1/4 inch thick
2 cups day-old bread, cubed
1/2 cup chopped unpared apple
2 oz. sharp natural cheddar cheese, shredded
2 T. raisins
2 T. chopped pecans
2 T. butter or margarine, melted
1/2 cup fresh orange juice
1/4 t. salt
1/8 t. ground cinnamon
1/4 t. fresh lemon peel
dash of nutmeg
1/2 cup water

Salt and pepper inside of pockets. Toss together bread, apple, cheese, raisins, and nuts. Combine melted butter, orange juice, salt, lemon peel, cinnamon and nutmeg; pour over bread-fruit mixture and mix gently. Stuff pork chops. Lightly brown both sides of chops in a hot Dutch oven. Place wire rack beneath pork chops, add water to bottom of the oven, bake at 350 F. for 3/4 to 1 hour.

Prepared by Ruesch Family
1988 Cookoff

PRESENTS

If you want to make the people you invite over to eat feel special, along with the great meal you will serve them, give them some kind of a little present. A small potpourri sachet, a small perfumed soap, a little bottle of homemade jam, or a little bottle of herbed vinegar that you have made.

Breads

Caraway Braided Bread

1 pkg. dry yeast
3/4 cup water, warm
2 T. sugar
1 t. salt
1 egg
1 T. vegetable flour
2 1/2-2 3/4 cups flour
1 egg yolk
2 T. cold water
caraway seeds

Dissolve yeast in warm water in large bowl. Stir in sugar, salt, 1 egg, 1 T. oil, and 1 1/4 cup flour. Beat until smooth. Stir in enough remaining flour to make dough easy to handle. Turn dough onto lightly floured surface; knead until smooth and elastic, about 5 minutes. Place in greased bowl; let rise in warm place until double, 1 1/2 to 2 hours. Punch down dough; divide into 3 equal parts. Roll each part into a rope, 14 inches long. Place ropes close together on lightly greased cookie sheet. Braid ropes together gently and loosely. Fasten ends; tuck under braid securely. Brush with oil. Let rise until double, 40 to 50 minutes. Heat oven to 375 F. Mix egg yolk and 2 T. water; brush braid with mixture. Sprinkle with caraway seeds. Bake until golden brown, 25 to 35 minutes.

Prepared by the Kinney Family 1988 Cookoff

Fabulous French Rolls

1 1/2 cups water
1 pkg. yeast (2 t.)
1 T. sugar
1 t. salt
2 T. butter or margarine
4 cups flour

Heat water in Dutch oven. Remove 1/2 cup at lukewarm stage and mix with yeast and sugar in separate bowl to dissolve. Set aside and let activate. Add salt and butter to hot water. In large mixing bowl, combine hot water mixture and 2 cups flour and beat until well blended. Add yeast mixture and 1 cup flour; mix, and add another cup of flour. Blend. Add more flour if necessary to make a moderately stiff dough. Knead until satiny and well mixed. Let raise for 1/2 hour. Punch down and form into balls. Dip balls into melted butter and place into Dutch oven. Sprinkle with sesame seeds. Cover and allow to raise until

SALADS

Salads make and excellent meal when combined with fresh homemade bread. Plan your breads and salads to compliment each other. This can be a lot of fun and great eating. Use fennel, watercress, endive, arugula, bibb lettuce, radish sprouts, spinach, different types of nuts,vegetables, fruits, and salad dressings to compliment the meal.

doubled in size. Bake with 6 briquets on the bottom and about fifteen on the top. Rotate oven 1/4 turn every 5 minutes. Butter the tops of the rolls when they are golden brown and serve with butter, honey or jam. Use a 12-inch Dutch oven. This recipe makes 12 rolls.

Prepared by Ruesch Family
1988 Cookoff

Hungarian Coffee Cake

Sweet Roll Dough recipe
1/2 cup margarine or butter, melted
1 T. ground cinnamon
1 1/3 cup sugar
3/4 cup chopped nuts

Shape dough into 1 1/2 inch balls. Dip into margarine, then into mixture of sugar, cinnamon and nuts. Place a single layer of balls in a well-greased 10-inch tube pan so they just touch. Top with another layer of balls. Let rise until double, about 40 minutes. Heat oven to 375 F. Bake until golden, brown, 35-40 minutes. (If it browns too quickly, cover loosely with foil). Loosen from pan. Immediately invert pan on serving plate. Let pan remain a minute so

"The most indispensable quality in a cook is punctuality, and no less is required of a guest."
-Brillat-Savarin

butter-sugar mixture can drizzle over coffee cake. To serve, break coffee cake apart with forks.

Sweet Roll Dough:
1 pkg. active dry yeast
1/2 cup warm water
1/2 cup lukewarm milk, scalded then cooled
1/3 cup sugar
1/3 cup shortening, margarine, or butter, softened
1 t. salt
1 egg
3 1/2 to 4 cups flour

Dissolve yeast in warm water in large bowl. Stir in milk, sugar, shortening, salt, egg, and 2 cups of the flour. Beat until smooth. Mix in enough remaining flour to make dough easy to handle. Turn dough onto lightly floured surface; knead until smooth and elastic, about 5 minutes. Place in greased bowl; turn greased side up. Cover; let rise in warm place until double, about 1 1/2 hours. (Dough is ready if an indentation remains when touched). Punch down dough. Shape, let rise and bake as directed.

Prepared by Anderton Family
1988 Cookoff

CREATIVE SAND-WICHES

Because there are so many different types of breads, there are many different combinations of sandwiches to tempt the appetite. Create them using breads, like italian, rye, pumpernickel, English muffins, sourdough, whole-wheat, white, and dill. Use sweet breads, like banana, cranberry, date and fig.

Karen's Cinnamon Rolls

2 cups scalded milk
1 cup sugar
2 t. salt
4 eggs beaten
3/4 cup melted butter
2 T. yeast
1/4 cup water
6 Cups flour

Dissolve yeast in luke warm water. Pour sugar, salt, yeast, eggs and shortening into milk. Beat well. Stir in flour. Let rest for 10 minutes. The dough will be sticky. Put on a floured board and knead until soft. Roll out to 3/4 inch thick. Add filling as desired.

Filling:
2 T. butter
1/2 cup brown sugar
1/2 cup raisins
1/4 cup chopped nuts
1 1/2 T. cinnamon

Frosting:
2 cups sifted powdered sugar
1/2 cup soft butter
1/4 t. vanilla
1/4 cup evaporated milk

Prepared by Steven Heward
1987 Cookoff

NUTS

Nuts can add a special texture and flavor to the dishes you may prepare. Try them at various times and see how well they blend with many dishes. Use pecans, peanuts, pine nuts, walnuts, macadamia nuts, hazelnuts, cashews, pistachios etc.

Orange-Cinnamon Sourdough Rolls

1 1/2 cup sourdough starter
4 cups flour (I used half wheat, half white)
4 t. baking powder
1 t. salt
1 cup buttermilk
1 t. soda dissolved in 1 T. water
1/2 cup butter, melted
1 cup sugar
2 T. grated orange peel
2 t. cinnamon
powdered sugar icing

Bring sourdough starter to room temperature. Sift together flour, baking powder and salt; set aside. Add buttermilk to starter, then stir in soda. Combine flour mixture with starter. Turn dough out onto a lightly floured surface; knead 15 times. Divide dough into two portions. Roll each portion into 12-inch square. Brush each square with 3 T. of the melted butter. Combine sugar, orange peel, and cinnamon; sprinkle over dough. Roll up, jelly roll style; seal seam. Slice each roll into 12 pieces; place up-side down, in a well greased 12-inch Dutch oven. Brush with remaining melted butter. Bake at 450 F. for 20-25 minutes or till golden. Immediately turn out onto Dutch oven lid; drizzle with

STORING FLOUR

Store whole-wheat flour, dark rye flour, pumpernickel and ryeflour in the refrigerator. Store other flours in tightly covered containers at room temperatures. If you need to keep them for a long period of time, you can freeze them.

powdered sugar icing. Makes 24.

Powdered Sugar Icing
Combine:
1 cup powdered sugar
1/2 t. vanilla
milk (enough for drizzling)

Prepared by the Jackson Family
1988 Cookoff

Quick Corn Bread

2 eggs
2 cups Bisquick
6 T. cornmeal
1 cup milk
1/2 t. soda
1/2 cup oil
2/3 cup sugar
3 T. Flour

Mix all ingredients together until they are a good consistency. Bake in a 9x9" pan, greased & floured or in muffin tins. This recipe will make 15-18 muffins. Bake at 400 F. for 30 minutes. Use 6-8 coals bottom and 18-20 coals top.

Prepared by Bill Davies
1987 Cookoff

ONION SMELL

You may have heard that the way to get the onion smell off of your hands, is to rub them with prepared mustard, like lotion, and then wash them with soap and water. If you are so inclined, try it. It really works. You may have a slight mustard smell, but this dissipates very rapidly. The onion smell on your hands lingers a long time!

Seven Week Bran Bread

1 cup nabisco 100% bran
1 cup boiling water
2 cups kelloggs 40% bran flakes
1/2 cup shortening
1 1/2 cups white sugar
2 eggs, beaten
2 1/2 cups flour
1/2 t. salt
2 1/2 t. baking soda
2 cups buttermilk
raisins, dates or nuts, (optional)

Soak bran in boiling water. Cream shortening with sugar. Add eggs, salt, soda and buttermilk. Mix together and add soaked bran. Add bran flakes. Mix until well blended. Bake at 350 F. for 30-40 minutes.

Prepared by Michael Treshow VII
1987 Cookoff

Sourdough Apricot Twists

1/2 cup milk
1 cup sourdough starter
1/4 cup vegetable oil
1 t. vanilla extract
3-4 cups all purpose flour
1/2 t. baking powder
1/4 t. baking soda
1 t. salt
1/3 cup sugar

GLUTEN

Bread flour is a specially developed flour with more protein or gluten, the substance that forms the structure in bread. It is not essential for success, but bread flour does make beautiful yeast breads. Bread flour can be substituted for all-purpose flour in recipes. If you do this expect to use less bread flour than all-purpose flour.

1 (8 oz.) pkg. cream cheese, softened
3/4 cup apricot jam
1 cup shredded coconut
1/2 cup chopped pecans
1/2 cup apricot jam (glaze)
Extra shredded coconut

In small saucepan (or Dutch oven) heat milk almost to a boil over medium heat. Do not boil. Set aside to cool (10 minutes). Generously grease a large baking sheet or use 14" dutch oven, set aside. In a large bowl, combine sourdough starter, cooled milk, oil and vanilla; set aside. In a medium bowl, combine 1 cup flour, baking powder, soda, salt and sugar. Stir into sourdough mixture. Stir in enough remaining flour to make a stiff dough. Turn out onto lightly floured surface. Knead about 2 minutes or until smooth and elastic. Preheat Dutch oven to about 375 F. Use 6-8 coals on bottom and 15-20 on top. Roll dough out to an 18" X 10" rectangle. Spread with softened cream cheese, then with 3/4 cup apricot jam. Sprinkle with 1 cup coconut and nuts. Fold rectangle in thirds lengthwise. Use a sharp knife to cut dough crosswise into 1" strips. Holding strips at each end, twist in opposite directions. Arrange twisted dough in Dutch

FROM THE CHEF'S NOTEBOOK

With this great recipe, you can try different fruit jams and different varieties of nuts to make a wonderful variety of twists.

oven, a few at a time. Bake for 20-25 minutes or until done. In a small saucepan, heat 1/2 cup apricot jam until warm. Remove twists and place them on a rack and brush with warmed jam. Decorate with shredded coconut, if desired. Makes about 18 twists.

Prepared by the Jager Family
1988 Cookoff

Sourdough Biscuits

2 cups flour
2 t. baking powder
1/4 t. soda
1/2 t. salt
3 t. sugar
1 cup sourdough starter

FROM THE CHEF'S NOTEBOOK

If you grow fresh herbs, and they are plentiful, use them around the house to freshen the air. They make beautiful additions to flower arrangements with their dark green and gray leaves.

Combine dry ingredients in a bowl, mixing well, then make a hole in the center and pour in the starter. Mix or knead in the bowl for several minutes. Pinch off golf ball size pieces and shape into biscuits. Place a little oil, melted butter, or bacon grease in a pie tin and dip both sides of each biscuit. Place in Dutch oven and set in a warm place to rise. Bake at 350 F. for 15 to 20 minutes.

Prepared by Paul Engel
1988 Cookoff

Sourdough Bread Sticks

Mix and dissolve in large bowl:
2 T. sugar
1 pkg. active dry yeast
1 1/2 cup hot water

Add:
1 cup sourdough start
1/2 t. salt
2 cups flour

Mix well for two minutes, then let sit and rest for 10 minutes.

Add:
1/2 t. soda
2 1/2 to 3 more cups of flour (as needed)

Mix well and continue kneading 5 to 10 minutes or until satiny in appearance. Place in greased bowl and let rise in warm spot until doubled in volume, knead down. Form into desired shape, brush on melted butter and sprinkle with 1/4 t. paprika mixed with 1/2 teaspoon garlic and parsley salt. Let rise until doubled. Bake for 35 to 45 minutes at 400 F.

Prepared by Bryan Harding & Ryan Larsen
1988 Cookoff

"Summer cooking implies a sense of immediacy, a capacity to capture the essence of the fleeting moment."
-Elizabeth David

Sourdough Cheese Rolls

1 T. yeast
1 1/2 t. salt
3 cups flour
1/2 t. baking soda
1/4 cup sugar
3/4 cup hot water
1 1/2 cup sourdough starter
1 egg
1/4 cup soft butter
1 cup grated sharp Cheddar cheese

Combine in a large bowl, yeast, flour, sugar, salt and baking soda. Melt butter in hot water. Mix in sourdough starter. Stir in egg. Stir into dry ingredients to make a soft dough. Stir well for 3-4 minutes. Mix in grated cheese. Turn out onto a floured canvas and knead 5-8 minutes or until smooth. Place in a greased bowl (turn dough to grease both sides). Cover and let rise until doubled. Punch down. Let rest 10 minutes. Divide into 24 pieces, shape into balls. Arrange balls in a greased 12" Dutch oven. Bake until golden brown.

Prepared by Cook family and Woods family
1988 Cookoff

FROM THE CHEF'S NOTEBOOK

When baking hard rolls or french breads, spread a thin layer of cornmeal in the bottom of the Dutch oven. This helps to prevent sticking.

Whole Wheat Currant Rolls

2 cups warm water
2 pkg dry yeast
3 T. oil
1 egg
1/2 cup sugar
1 cup dried currants
1 T. Salt
4 t. cinnamon
6 to 7 cups whole wheat flour

Put yeast in water and dissolve. In large bowl add 5 cups flour, salt, cinnamon and sugar. Mix well. Add yeast mixture, oil, egg and currants. Mix with spoon adding flour until mixture can be kneaded with hands. Knead and form into smooth ball (about 10 minutes) that is not sticky. Lightly oil and form into rolls. Place in lightly oiled 12 inch Dutch oven. Let raise until doubled in size about 1 hour. Bake 5 to 8 coals bottom, 14-16 coals top for 35-40 minutes.

Prepared by Val and Marie Cowley
1988 Cookoff

Whole Wheat Quick Bread

1 egg, beaten
2 cups buttermilk
3 T molasses or honey
1 1/2 T. melted butter

TEMPERATURES

-10 F. = Freezer storage

32 F. = Water freezes

68 F. = Room temperature

205 F. = Water simmers

212 F. = Water boils

2 cups whole wheat flour
1 t. soda
1 t. salt
1 t. baking powder
1/2 cup raisins

Combine egg, buttermilk, molasses, and melted butter, then stir in dry ingredients that have been mixed together. Stir in raisins, and spoon batter into two greased loaf pans. Bake at 400 F. for about 1 hour.

Prepared by the Varsity Scouts 1988 Cookoff

Desserts

Apple pie

Pie Filling:
10 big apples, peeled & sliced
2 pie crust
1/2 cube butter
2 T. cinnamon
1 T. sugar

Topping:
1 cup shredded cheddar cheese
1/2 cup brown sugar

Line Dutch oven with pie crusts, on bottom and up the sides. Fill crust with sliced apples, cinnamon

FROM THE CHEF'S NOTEBOOK

When planning a meal, be sure that you have plenty. It is always better to have a little too much, than too little and have people go away unsatisfied.

and sugar over apples. Dot with butter. Spread topping over apples. Bake in 12" Dutch oven 55 minutes or until done. 6-8 coals on bottom, 14-16 coals top.

Prepared by Bob Kinney
1987 Cookoff

Bear Lake Berry Cake

Mix together:
1 box pound cake mix
Pour batter in 8x8x2 cake pan
Sprinkle on top of batter
2 cups fresh raspberries
bake at 325 for 30-45 minutes. Place cake pan on rack inside Dutch oven. 6-7 coals bottom, 12-14 coals top.

Prepared by Michael Treshow VII
1987 Cookoff

Blueberry Pie

Crust:
2 cups flour
1 cup shortening
1 t. salt
1 t. sugar
4-6 T. water

Mix flour and salt in mixing bowl. Cut in shortening till mixture is

CHOCOLATE COVERED FRUITS

If you want to try something delicious, try coating some of your favorite fruits with chocolate. Melt a semisweet or sweet chocolate bar, broken into pieces, over a low heat. If possible, leave stems on the fruits. Use strawberries, raspberries, cherries, grapes, tangerine and orange sections, bananas, apples or pears. Dip the fruit into the chocolate. With a toothpick, secure the piece of fruit and place it up-side-down, sticking the toothpick in a piece of styrofoam. This will allow the chocolate to dry.

crumbly. Add water and stir with fork. Knead till manageable.

Pie Filling:
4 Cups fresh or frozen blueberries
3/4 cup sugar
2 T. flour
2 T. cornstarch
1/2 t. salt
1 T. lemon juice
1/4 t. grated lemon rind

Line 9" pie pan with pastry. Mix blueberries with remaining ingredients. Place in pie pan, dot with butter. Roll out top crust, adjust and seal. Bake at 400 F. for 45-60 minutes. Cool and enjoy.

Prepared by Anderton Famliy
1988 Cookoff

Caramel Pudding Cake

Syrup:
2 cups packed brown sugar
3 cups water
2 T. butter or margarine

In Dutch oven, combine ingredients to make syrup and bring to boil. Pour into separate container and set aside.

Batter:
3 T. shortening

FROM THE CHEF'S NOTEBOOK

If you have everything prepared in advance of the arrival of your guests, try to have an aroma like something is still cooking. With Dutch oven cooking, sometimes, all you have to do, is leave one of the lids ajar. The smell has a very welcoming effect.

1 t. vanilla
3/4 t. salt
1 1/2 t. soda
2 cups raisins
1 cup chopped nuts
1 1/2 cups sugar
3 cups flour
1 t. cinnamon
1 1/2 cups milk
1 cup water

In a mixing bowl cream shortening and sugar. Add vanilla. Sift dry ingredients together and add to creamed mixture, alternating with milk. In Dutch oven boil raisins in water to soften. Stir raisins with water (do not drain raisins) and nuts into batter. Pour into 12" Dutch oven. Pour syrup over batter. Bake at 350 F. for 30-45 minutes. Serve scoops upside-down so caramel sauce runs over cake.

Prepared by Ruesch Family
1988 Cookoff

Chocolate Pudding Cake

Pudding:
1 cup brown sugar
2 cups water
1/2 cup cocoa
1 cup miniature marshmallows

BITTER-SWEET SEMISWEET

Often times people confuse bittersweet chocolate with unsweetened and semisweet chocolate. Bittersweet contains less sugar than semisweet and is mainly used in baking. When a recipe calls for bittersweet, that is what you should use. Don't substitute unless you know how to make the proper adjustments.

Mix brown sugar and cocoa, add water and stir until well blended. Add mixture over miniature marshmallows.

Cake:
1 1/2 cups sugar
1/2 cup cocoa
3/4 cup shortening
1/4 t. salt
2 eggs
2 1/4 cups flour
1 1/2 t. baking soda
3/4 cup milk
3/4 cup boiling water
1 1/2 t. vanilla

Mix sugar, cocoa, shortening, and salt. Add egg, beat well. Sift flour with soda, and add alternately with milk, boiling water, and vanilla. Blend until smooth. Place pudding mixture in Dutch oven, and spoon cake mixture over the top of the pudding. Top with chopped nuts, cover and bake for 40-50 minutes.

Prepared by Varsity Scouts
1988 Cookoff

Cookie Apple Cobbler

6 cups sliced apples
3/4 cup brown sugar
2 T. flour

FROM THE CHEF'S NOTEBOOK

Some great easy desserts during the summer are: lemon and orange halves filled with ice cream; peaches and heavy cream; strawberries covered with white or dark chocolate; melons hollowed out and filled with other fruits, or ice cream or jello.

1 1/2 t. cinnamon
Dash fresh grated nutmeg
1 1/2 T. lemon juice

Combine ingredients and place in greased, foil lined 10" Dutch oven. Top with sugar cookie dough.

Sugar Cookie Dough

3/4 cup sugar
1/3 cup butter
1 egg beaten
1 T. milk
1 1/2 cups flour
1 1/4 t. baking powder
1/4 t. salt
1/2 t. vanilla

Combine sugar and butter. Add egg, milk and vanilla. Sift dry ingredients together. Beat into creamed mixture. Chill till ready to top apples. Pat dough into 10 inch circle and place on top of apple mixture. Combine 1 T. sugar and 1/4 t. cinnamon. Sprinkle on dough. Bake 30-40 minutes until golden brown. Top with whipped cream if desired.

Prepared by Cook family and Woods family
1988 Cookoff

GIANT COOKIES

Giant cookies are a favorite of almost everyone. Make your favorite cookie recipe. Choose an average-size ice cream scoop for portioning the dough. Drop the dough into the bottom of your well-greased oven. You may have room for 2-3 cookies, depending on the size of your oven. Wet your hand with water and push the dough into a 4-5-inch round. Bake as directed.

Fresh Peach Dumplings

3 peaches (skinned & seeded)
1 egg
1 t. water

Beat egg and water together

Filling: mix together and fill peaches
1/4 cup currants
2 T. slivered almonds
1/4 cup brown sugar
1/4 t. nutmeg
1/4 t. cinnamon

Sauce: mix together
1 1/2 cups hot water
3/4 cup sugar
1/2 t. cinnamon
3 T. butter or margarine
1/2 t. nutmeg

Crust:
2 cups flour
1 t. salt
2/3 cup lard
5 to 7 T. cold water

Sift flour and salt together. Cream in lard with pastry cutter until mixture is the size of small peas. Sprinkle 1 T. at a time cold water over mixture. Gently tossing each time with fork. Continue until all is moistened and forms ball. Divide into thirds and form balls.

PEACHES

Peaches are the most widely grown fruit tree in the world next to the apple. It is wonderful to use in numerous dishes.

Roll out ball and cut to form 8" triangle. Place filled peach in center and gently pinch sides together. Brush dough with beaten egg and water mixture. Place in Dutch oven and bake. 10 coals on bottom and 20 coals on top for 15 minutes. Then remove 5 coals from bottom and 6 coals from top and pour sauce over dumplings. Bake for 45 minutes more, basting occasionally. Dumplings should be browned on top but pastry will be dumpling like on bottom.

Prepared by the Cowley Family 1988 Cookoff

Grandma's Apple Pie

5 large tart apple, peeled, cored, and sliced (about 5 cups)
1 c. sugar
1 T. lemon juice
2 T. flour
1/8 t. salt
1/2 t. cinnamon
1/2 t. nutmeg
1 T. butter
pastry for double crust pie
sugar

Combine all ingredients except butter and let stand while preparing pastry. Line 10" Dutch

FROM THE CHEF'S NOTEBOOK

You can make excellent puddings in the Dutch oven. Try you favorite: vanilla, chocolate, butterscotch, peanut butter, coconut etc.

oven with pastry; add filling and dot with butter. Cover with rolled dough for top crust. Seal and flute edges; then sprinkle crust with sugar. Make slits to allow steam to escape. Bake for 15 minutes at 450 F.; then reduce temperature to 350 F. and bake for 35-45 minutes, or until crust is golden.

No-fail Pie Crust

2 1/2 cups sifted flour
1 t. salt
1 cup shortening
1/4 c. cold water
1 T. vinegar
1 egg, beaten

Sift together flour and salt. Cut in half of shortening until mixture resembles small peas; then cut in rest of shortening until mixture resembles navy beans. In a mixing bowl combine water, vinegar and egg. Pour into flour mixture and mix lightly with fork until all flour is moistened and pastry forms a ball. Divide pastry into two portions - approximately 2/3 for bottom crust and 1/3 for top crust. Roll out between waxed paper.

Prepared by Jackson Family
1988 Cookoff

"Nothing is really work unless you'd rather be doing something else."
-Peter Pan, James Barrie

Peach Raspberry Flan

1 1/2 cup flour
1/2 t. salt
1/2 cup shortening
3-4 T. water
4-6 peaches, thinly sliced
1/2 cup raspberries
1 cup sugar
6 eggs, slightly beaten
1 pt. heavy cream
3 t. vanilla
1/4 t. salt

Mix flour, salt, shortening, and water, to make pie dough. Roll pie dough to 10 inch diameter. Line Flan pan or Springform pan with pie dough. Place in 350 F. oven 10 - 15 minutes, until golden. Brush shell with egg white; cook 2 more minutes. Remove and cool. Half peaches and cut into thin wedges; line pie shell. Arrange top layer of peaches in pinwheel fashion. Place raspberries in center. Mix eggs, sugar, heavy cream, vanilla, and salt; gently pour over peaches. Place in 350 F. and bake for 1 hour or until knife inserted in pie comes out clean. If flan is not to be served immediately it is recommended to melt some apricot preserves and brush over the top.

Prepared by Kinney Family
1988 Cookoff

FROM THE CHEF'S NOTEBOOK

You can make and excellent drink by filling a glass one- third full of raspberry vinegar. Add ice, a teaspoon of honey and fill the rest of the way with carbonated water. Add fresh raspberries and a sprig of mint. This also works great with blueberries and strawberries.

Pioneer Carrot Cake

2 cups flour
2 t. soda
2 t. cinnamon
1/2 t. salt
2 t. vanilla
1 8 oz. can crushed pineapple, drained
2 cup grated carrots
1 1/2 cups flaked coconut
1 cup coarsely chopped walnuts or pecans
3 eggs
3/4 cup vegetable oil
3/4 cup buttermilk
2 cup sugar

Grease and flour 14" Dutch oven. Sift together first 4 ingredients, set aside.   Beat eggs and add oil, buttermilk, sugar and vanilla, mix well.   Add   flour   mixture, pineapple, carrots, coconut and nuts; mix well. Pour batter into pan. Bake for 55 minutes or until toothpick comes out clean.

Cream Cheese Frosting

3 cups powdered sugar
12 oz. cream cheese
1 t. evaporated milk
1 t. vanilla

Prepared by Steven Heward
1987 Cookoff

VANILLA

One of the most familiar flavorings in our everyday foods is vanilla. It comes from a rare species of the orchid family. A suitable bean is produced on only a single day once a year. If that day is missed, a whole year must pass before another bean can be harvested. Artificial vanilla can be made, but the flavor can't compare to the real thing.

Rhubarb Cobbler

*1 1/2 cups fresh, sweetened
rhubarb*
1 1/2 cups water
1/2 cup sugar
1 cup biscuit mix
1/3 cup milk

Cook rhubarb in water for 5 minutes. Place mixture in lightly greased Dutch oven, preheated over the coals. Combine sugar, biscuit mix and milk. Stir until dough holds together. Drop biscuit dough by spoonfuls onto hot rhubarb. Place lid on oven and cover with hot coals. Cook for about 15-20 minutes.

Basic Biscuit Mix
8 cups flour
8 t. baking powder
4 t. salt
1 t. sugar
1 1/2 cups shortening

Mix thoroughly flour, baking powder, salt and sugar. Cut in shortening with pastry cutter or mix with hands until texture of fine crumbs.

Prepared by Paul Engel
1988 Cookoff

FREEZING RHUBARB

If you would like to freeze rhubarb when it is plentiful, so you will have it to use all summer, cut stalks into 1/2-inch pieces, diced. Place them in airtight freezer bags, and freeze. You can then use them frozen in many dishes, or stew them with some sugar.

Sourdough   Bavarian Apple Torte

Crust:
1/2 cup butter or margarine
1/2 cup sugar
2 t. soda
1 t. vanilla
1/2 cup sourdough start
2 cups flour

Cream butter and vanilla. Stir in start. Add the soda to the flour then add it to the butter, sugar and start mix. Mix until smooth. cover the bottom and about 1/2 inch up the sides of a torte pan that fits in your oven, with this soft dough.

Cream Cheese Layer:
8 oz. cream cheese
1/4 cup sugar
1 egg
1/2 t. vanilla

Beat the cheese, sugar, egg, and vanilla until smooth then spread it over the dough.

Apple Layer:
1/2 cup sugar
1 t. cinnamon
1/2 t. nutmeg
1 20 oz. bottle sliced apples
1/4 cup sliced almonds

Combine the sugar and cinnamon

FRUIT SALADS

When fruit is plentiful, don't use a recipe for your salad. Just pick those fruits you want, and combine them together. Use different flavored mayonnaises and fruit juices for the sauce. You can create some wonderful fruit salads. Remember that fresh mint goes great with fruits.

in a small bowl. Drain the juice from the apples and then add the sugar to the apples. Stir until the apples are coated with the sugar and cinnamon mix. Spread over the cheese mixture and sprinkle with almonds. Bake at 400 degrees for 20 minutes. Let cool before removing from pan, unless you like hot apple pie. This recipe from the book Sourdough Cooking by Dean Tucker.

Prepared by Lynn R. Ertmann
1988 Cookoff

Toasted Butter Pecan Cake

2 cups pecans, chopped
1 1/4 cups butter
3 cups sifted flour
2 t. baking powder
1/2 t. salt
2 cups sugar
4 unbeaten eggs
1 cup milk
2 t. vanilla

Toast pecans in 1/4 cup butter in bottom of Dutch oven. Stir frequently. Sift flour with baking powder and salt. Cream 1 cup butter, gradually add sugar, creaming well, blend in eggs, beat well after each. Add dry

"I prefer the errors of enthusiasm to the indifference of wisdom."
-Anatole France

FROM THE CHEF'S NOTEBOOK

You can make a lot of different up-side-down cakes. All you have to do is follow the same directions for the pineapple up-side-down cake and substitute different fruits, and different cake mixes. These are a lot of fun. People really like the up-side-down cakes. Try it with apples, and a spice cake, or pears and and white cake with cinnamon red-hots mixed in it.

ingredients alternating with milk, beginning and ending with dry ingredients. Blend well after each addition. Stir in vanilla and 1 1/3 cups pecans. Turn into Dutch oven that has been greased and floured. Bake at 350 F. for 40-50 minutes. 5 coals on bottom and 15 on top. Adjust heat - take off coals except 4-5 small coals on top to finish baking for 10-15 minutes more.

Butter Pecan Frosting

Cream 1/4 cup butter
Add 1 lb. powdered sugar, sifted
1 t. vanilla
4-6 T. evaporated milk
Stir in remaining pecans, frost cake.

Prepared by Jager family
1988 Cookoff

Don't be afraid to be creative when preparing the foods you are making. Above is pictured a cow by a barn on the crust of this Hearty Beef Pie (page 138).

INDEX TO RECIPES

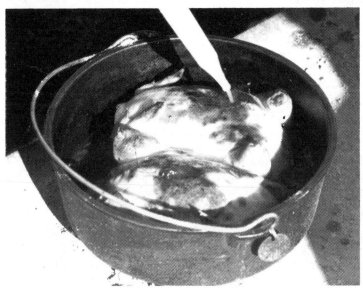

Basting is appropriate on many of the dishes you will prepare.